Contents

Foreword   5

Introduction   7

B2 Reading

- Part 5 Multiple choice   13
- Part 6 Gapped text   21
- Part 7 Multiple matching   29
- Practice tests   39
- Answers   73

B2 Listening

- Part 1 Multiple choice   105
- Part 2 Sentence completion   111
- Part 3 Multiple matching   117
- Part 4 Multiple choice   121
- Practice tests   127
- Answers   161
- Transcripts   195

Let's Go Cambridge!
Practice makes perfect

Fiona Aish, Simon Haines and Jo Tomlinson

B2 First

Preparation for

Reading

Listening

JoEnglish

© Prosperity Education Ltd. 2025

Registered offices: Sherlock Close, Cambridge
CB3 0HP, United Kingdom

First published 2025

ISBN: 978-1-915654-30-4

This publication is in copyright. Subject to statutory exception and to the provisions of relevant collective licensing agreements, no reproduction of any part may take place without the written permission of Prosperity Education.

The moral right of the author has been asserted.

'Cambridge B2 First' and 'FCE' are brands belonging to The Chancellor, Masters and Scholars of the University of Cambridge and are not associated with Prosperity Education or JoEnglish.

Designed by ORP Cambridge

For further information and resources, visit:
www.prosperityeducation.net

To infinity and beyond.

Foreword

Hello, everyone. How are you?

My name is Joe Sanders, better known online as 'JoEnglish', and it is with great pleasure and pride that I present this book, which in my opinion is the best and most focused B2 First (FCE) preparation resource available. But who am I? What gives me the right to say this?

I started my teaching journey in 2005, when I gained my PGCE and began teaching in state schools in England. I taught for two years in Oxford before moving with my wife Marielena to Italy, where we opened a language school in Locorotondo, Puglia. The school proved a great success through which we prepared hundreds of students for the whole suite of Cambridge exams. The success rate amongst our students was exceptional, as we concentrated on what makes not only a successful student but also a successful teacher. Without the right guidance, passing an exam like the B2 First is extremely difficult.

To gain a deeper insight into the exams, I became a speaking examiner for Cambridge in 2012. This experience enabled me to understand precisely what Cambridge is looking for in their candidates and gain invaluable information that I could pass on to my own students.

Having moved on from the school in Puglia, I now run my YouTube channel 'JoEnglish' and other social media pages on Instagram, Facebook and Tiktok. To my delight, I have a combined following of more than 1 million students, many of whom are preparing for Cambridge exams. In 2021 I opened my website JoEnglish.com, which offers a complete online English language learning experience. It was in setting up this website that I first worked with Prosperity Education. In need of top-quality exam-preparation materials to complement my Cambridge courses, they had exactly what I wanted, and so together we have been helping students reach their goal of achieving success in the Cambridge exams. The partnership works really well: high-quality material written by experienced authors and reviewed independently by assessment experts combined with my 20 years of exam-teaching experience makes for a comprehensive exam-preparation student journey.

The content I have selected for this book comes from the *Cambridge Masterclass* series by Prosperity Education, authored by: **Simon Haines**, an ELT writer, teacher and teacher trainer who has written a wide range of course books, skills materials and teacher handbooks. He is co-author of the coursebook *Landmark* (OUP) and exam titles *First Masterclass* (OUP), *IELTS Masterclass* (OUP) and *Complete Advanced* (CUP); **Fiona Aish** and **Jo Tomlinson** are both DELTA-qualified and hold MAs in ELT and Applied Linguistics and Language Testing, respectively. Together, they have written several leading titles in English exam preparation, both for Cambridge English examinations and IELTS.

You may be thinking 'why put Reading and Listening together as sub skills when usually Reading and Writing are put together?' I know that's the norm, but it doesn't mean it always has to be this way! Let me explain the reasoning behind this...

Reading and Listening naturally go together. I always tell my students that when listening they should also read the transcript to really understand how we pronounce words and use connected speech. This allows for both skills to be practised together and helps to improve reading skills whilst listening: it forces you to read at a quicker pace, which is invaluable during the exam when you have to read large texts under the pressure of time constraints. Another important benefit to combining these sub skills is understanding how these exam questions are structured. In the Reading and Listening parts of the exam, the way in which the questions are presented is in fact very similar, unlike in the Writing parts where they are completely different. By studying Reading and Listening together, you are continually reinforcing important exam techniques that complement oneanother.

Remember, passing a Cambridge exam is as much a test of technique as it is of your English level. Throughout this book you will receive tips to help you pass the exam using the correct techniques, and the accompanying exam-styled practice tests aim to reinforce this learning.

So, are you ready?

Let's go Cambridge!

Introduction

B2 First is one of the exams in the series provided by Cambridge Assessment – part of the University of Cambridge. It is the second in the range of tests they provide in General English:

A2	Key (KET)
B1	Preliminary (PET)
B2	First (FCE)
C1	Advanced (CAE)
C2	Proficiency (CPE)

The references next to each test refer to the CEFR Level (Common European Framework of Reference), and show the language level of each test.

Cambridge B2 First Reading

For CEFR B2 Reading, you will need to be able to:

- understand the structure and development of a text

- deal confidently with a variety of types of text

- understand the gist or general idea and purpose of a text

- understand specific information: main ideas and details

- understand the opinions and attitudes of the writer

- understand the tone of the text (tone can relate to the writer's mood or to the emotions they are trying to express)

- understand the implications of what you read (implications are ideas that are suggested but not stated directly)

- understand the links between various parts of a text, for example between sentences and paragraphs (this involves understanding words and phrases like these: *however, whereas, what's more, in other words*).

How does the Reading test work?

You can take the B2 First exam on a computer or on paper. The content is the same for both forms of the test. The Reading section of the B2 First Reading and Use of English papers

give you the opportunity to show your comprehension and reading ability with different types of text, such as fiction, newspapers and magazines, letters and emails. The B2 First Reading and Use of Engish paper consists of the following:

Time allowed	1 hour 15 minutes
Number of parts	7
Number of questions	**Parts 1–4**: Use of English (these parts focus on your knowledge of grammar and vocabulary) **Parts 5–7**: Reading • Part 5: six multiple-choice questions • Part 6: six gapped-text questions • Part 7: ten multiple-matching questions

There is more information to process in the Reading parts of this paper, so it is advisable to allow a little more than half the time for Parts 5–7.

Part 5: Multiple choice

This part of the B2 First Reading examination consists of a text followed by six multiple-choice questions. For each question there are four options: A, B, C or D. There are 2 marks for each correct answer.

These questions check your ability to:

- read for detail

- recognise the tone of the text

- understand the attitude and opinions of the writer

- understand the main idea and purpose of the text

- understand the implications of what you read.

Part 6: Gapped text

This part of the examination consists of a single page of text with six numbered gaps. These gaps represent missing sentences. After the text, there are the six missing sentences and one extra sentence that does not fit into the text. These sentences are not in the right order according to the text. You have to read the text and the sentences to decide which sentence best fits each gap and which sentence is not needed. There are 2 marks for each correct answer. This part checks your ability to:

- understand the structure and development of a text

- make thematic connections between the missing sentences and the text

- recognise connecting words that link the text and the missing sentences (these may include pronouns, like *he* or *she*, determiners like *this* or *these*, or linking words like *however* or *therefore*)

- recognise key words in both the sentences before and after the gaps

- find linguistic evidence for your choice of answers.

Part 7: Multiple matching

This part of the examination consists of a series of questions followed by several short texts or a single longer text divided into paragraphs or sections. You have to match each question to a text or to the section of a text in which you can find the information. There is 1 mark for each correct answer.

Part 7 checks your ability to:

- skim a text for gist or general understanding

- read or scan a text for specific information

- notice textual clues while you scan

- understand the opinion and attitude of the writer

- locate detail in a large amount of text quickly.

Cambridge B2 First Listening

For CEFR B2 Listening, you will need to be able to:

- understand the topic or the purpose of the extract

- identify the overall meaning of the extract or specific details

- identify how speakers feel or their attitude towards a topic or situation

- understand when two speakers agree or disagree.

How does the Listening test work?

You can take the B2 First exam on a computer or on paper. The content is the same for both forms of the test. The Listening section of the B2 First examination gives you the opportunity

to show your comprehension ability by following a range of spoken materials, including news programmes, presentations and everyday conversations.

The B2 First Listening paper consists of the following:

Time allowed	40 minutes
Number of parts	4
Number of questions	Part 1: eight multiple-choice questions Part 2: ten sentence-completion questions Part 3: eight multiple-matching questions Part 4: seven multiple-choice questions

Part 1: Multiple choice

This first part of the B2 First Listening examination consists of eight short extracts, which could be monologues or dialogues. Each extract has one multiple-choice question with three options: A, B or C. There is one mark for each correct answer. You will listen to each extract twice.

These questions test your ability to:

- understand the topic or the purpose of the extract

- identify the overall meaning of the extract or specific details

- identify how speakers feel or their attitude towards a topic or situation

- understand when two speakers agree or disagree.

Part 2: Sentence completion

The second part of the B2 First Listening examination consists of one longer extract of 3–4 minutes, which is a monologue. You must complete ten sentences about this extract. Complete the gaps with words you hear on the recording. There is one mark for each correct answer. You will listen to each extract twice.

These questions test your ability to:

- understand detail

- identify specific information

- identify the speaker's opinion

- follow longer speech.

Part 3: Multiple matching

Part 3 of the B2 First Listening examination consists of five short monologues of about 30 seconds. All the speakers will talk about the same topic but from a different point of view. You have to match what each speaker says to a list of options. There are eight options so three are not needed. There is one mark for each correct answer. You will listen to each extract twice.

These questions test your ability to:

- understand detail; identify specific information
- understand different speakers
- identify different opinions and feelings.

Part 4: Multiple choice

The final part of the B2 First Listening examination consists of one longer extract of 3–4 minutes, which is a dialogue between two speakers. There are seven multiple-choice questions about the extract. These will follow the order of the information you hear. The questions each have three options: A, B or C. There is one mark for each correct answer. You will listen to each extract twice.

These questions test your ability to:

- understand main ideas and identify specific information
- identify the speaker's opinion and attitude
- follow longer speech.

How to use this book

The main section of this book focuses on each Reading and Listening task type individually, explaining its characteristics and providing guidance on how to plan a response to an example question. There follow several exam-styled practice tests with detailed answer keys and commentary. Each unit contains the following sections:

- **Prepare:** This section introduces the question type, describes what you are are being tested on and gives you guidance and detailed suggestions to help you do well.
- **Practise:** To prepare you for taking on an exam-styled text and questions, each unit contains a series of practice exercises with detailed answer keys that clarify how and

why answers are correct. These exercises are shorter than the real exam, but follow the same format.

- **Put it to the test:** Next there are two full-length exam-styled texts with questions. Again, there are detailed answer keys. You will find these keys especially helpful as they explain why the correct answers are correct as well as point out why you may have chosen incorrect answers (such as 'distractors').

Answers and transcripts

Detailed answers to questions for each unit are provided along with full transcripts of each audio recording.

Practice tests

The resource contains an additional eight B2 First Reading and Listening practice tests with audio, transcripts and answer keys.

Audio download

To access or download the audio content, visit:

www.prosperityeducation.net/downloads

- Select book image
- Enter password: **JOENGLISH**

B2 First Reading

Part 5: Multiple choice

Prepare

This part of the B2 First Reading examination consists of a text followed by six multiple-choice questions. For each question there are four options: A, B, C or D. There are 2 marks for each correct answer. These questions check your ability to:

- read for detail

- recognise the tone of the text (tone can relate to the writer's mood or to the emotions they are trying to make readers feel)

- understand the attitude and opinions of the writer

- understand the main idea and purpose of the text

- understand the implications of what you read (implications are ideas that are suggested but not stated directly).

Suggestions to help you do well in this task

- **Do not** begin by reading the whole text. Doing so will take time, and there is no need: each question is presented in the same order as its answer appears in the text, and often, each question is linked to a single paragraph.

- The four options can be confusing as they are often very similar and contain 'distractors' – pieces of information that may lead you towards choosing the wrong answer. So… **don't** read the four options! To begin with, just read the question and then start reading the text until you find the part that seems to refer to the question. You should then have an idea of the answer.

- Next, start checking the options… but **don't** just look for the correct answer! It is important to use deduction. Exclude each option until you only have one left. Then underline in the text where the correct answer is. If you can't underline the answer in this way, it usually isn't the answer!

- Repeat this process for the following questions. It's important to underline the answers in the text so that, if you have time at the end to check your work, you can find them quickly.

Have a go at some practice questions on the following pages.

JoEnglish Let's Go Cambridge! B2 First Reading and Listening

Practise

You are going to read four extracts from an article about the World's Strongest Man Competition. For each question, choose the answer A, B, C or D that you think fits best according to the text.

Extract 1

Preparing for the World's Strongest Man Competition is a demanding process, but it's also a rewarding one. First of all, I have to consume a lot of calories to fuel my training. I usually eat around 8,000-to-10,000 calories per day, relying on a diet that's high in protein-rich foods like lean meat, fish and eggs, carbohydrates and healthy fats. I also have to eat frequently throughout the day to reach my calorie goal, so I'm constantly snacking on things like nuts and berries in between multiple large meals.

***

Q. What does the writer say about his preparation for the competition?

- A He has to avoid eating too many snacks.
- B He must follow a strict diet.
- C He needs to eat rich food.
- D He has to eat at specific times of the day.

Extract 2

Building up almost super-human strength requires intense weightlifting and functional fitness exercises. I train for several hours a day, six days a week, and I focus on exercises that will help me perform well in the competition.

It's important to take care of your body while training, and I make sure to warm up properly before each workout, stretch regularly and take it easy on the days when I'm feeling particularly tired or sore. At the same time, it's essential to push yourself to reach your goals.

***

Q. In these two paragraphs, the writer explains

- A that he never allows himself to relax while he is training.
- B that he concentrates solely on increasing his strength.
- C that his training exercises are always painful.
- D how he trains for the competition without damaging his body.

Extract 3

Preparation for the competition requires a great deal of dedication and sacrifice, and I've had to give up some of my social life and devote all of my time and energy to training. It can also be difficult to maintain relationships with friends and family who don't understand the time and dedication required to compete at this level. But I'm lucky: I have a network of people who understand and support my goals.

***

Q. What does the writer say about his personal relationships while he is training?

- **A** He spends no time with friends while he is training.
- **B** It's impossible for him to stay on good terms with people.
- **C** There is a group of people who are sympathetic to his aims.
- **D** He feels fortunate to have family support for what he is doing.

Extract 4

It also costs a fortune. There are gym memberships, supplements and equipment, as well as the high cost of travel from Iceland to many different competition venues and expensive accommodation for the competition. I mean, it's great to see the world while I'm competing, but it does come at a cost; I have given up a lot so I wouldn't miss out. But I have made up my mind to give my all to make it to the competition, and I believe it's worth it.

Of course, I couldn't do any of this without the support of my sponsors. It's vital to have a solid brand and a strong and constant social media presence. This allows you to showcase your achievements, training and personality to a wider audience and, for some competitors, attract potential sponsors.

***

Q. What does the writer say about the costs involved in entering competitions?

- **A** The main expense involved is travelling all over the world.
- **B** He doubts whether going in for this competition is good value for money.
- **C** He spends a lot on money on creating his profile on social media.
- **D** He is dependent on the financial support he gets from others.

JoEnglish Let's Go Cambridge! B2 First Reading and Listening

Put it to the test 1

You are going to read an extract from a blog post in which a professional gamer – someone who gets paid for playing video games – describes his work. For questions 31–36, read the text below and decide which answer fits best according to the text. For each question, mark the appropriate answer (A, B, C or D).

I remember when I first started playing computer games. It was back when I was just a kid, and my parents had gotten me a second-hand video games console for my birthday. I would rush home from school and spend hours on end playing games, as did a lot of children in my friend group, and I quickly became obsessed with them. My brother was the opposite and couldn't stand them. As I got older, I realised that gaming was more than just a hobby for me – it was a passion.

That's how I ended up gaming professionally. It wasn't an easy decision to make, and I thought long and hard about it, but I knew that I had the skills to compete at a high level. I have to admit that it took a lot of effort to persuade my parents to take it seriously, but their opinion meant more to me than any opinion of my friends. My father wasn't pleased when I told him my plan was to keep on playing games in my bedroom! I started competing in local tournaments, and as I gained more experience and success I decided to take my talents to the next level.

As a professional gamer, I earn money in various ways such as from winning tournament prizes, advertising money from streaming my games on websites such as Twitch or YouTube (plus online videos talking about the games) and even donations from fans. My dream would be for a big company to sponsor me, but that's a long way off. This industry is growing rapidly, and the potential for earning money as a professional gamer is increasing. However, it requires commitment, talent and hard work to succeed in this competitive field. And I'm 100% committed – I couldn't imagine doing anything else.

Nowadays, my days are a balancing act between practising, streaming my games to my audience, responding to comments from my followers and taking breaks to avoid getting too tired. When I get into my game setup in the morning, I fill out my schedule for the day – I might spend a few hours practising for the next competition, reviewing past games or taking part in online tournaments.

Despite how much I love gaming, there are times when I do get bored of it. Some people get addicted to video games, and it can be hard for them to step away from the screen. But when I feel that way, I know it's time to quit for a while and focus on something else. The cycling helps with this, but I also like to read or do some drawing.

The choice of which game to play can depend on various factors such as personal preference, skill level and the current popularity of a game. Some games can make professionals more money than others – financially, the big multi-player battle games are the ones to get into. As for my personal favourite, it's hard to choose just one. There are so many incredible games out there, each with their unique strengths and weaknesses. However, I have a particular love for League of Monsters and all the games that made me try competitive gaming.

Looking to the future, I have high hopes for my gaming career. I want to keep improving my skills, win more competitions and inspire others to follow their passions. The next step for me will be to get some sponsors, and I know that this will take a lot of hard work.

It takes a lot of nerve to pursue a career in gaming, but I know it will be worth it.

31. How did the author get into gaming?

    A   by playing a lot of games after school with his friends
    B   by playing on a used gaming system he received
    C   by playing online games with his parents
    D   by playing online games with his brother

32. What does the author say about his decision to become a professional gamer?

    A   He made the choice very quickly.
    B   His parents fully supported him.
    C   His friends helped him to make the choice.
    D   It took him a long time to decide.

33. What does the author do to make money from gaming?

    A   He has yet to make money.
    B   He is sponsored by a major brand.
    C   He relies on his fans to pay him.
    D   He has several sources of income.

34. In line 21, what does 'my days are a balancing act' mean?

    A   The author feels the pressure to perform for his fans.
    B   The author has to manage many things simultaneously.
    C   The author has days where he has to do competitions and promotion.
    D   The author needs to manage gaming and another job.

35. In the fifth paragraph, the author talks about gaming and says that he

    A   doesn't enjoy it as much as he used to.
    B   thinks he will probably need to quit gaming soon.
    C   usually enjoys it but sometimes it's not so much fun.
    D   knows he has quite a heavy addiction to it.

36. Which games does the author say are his favourites?

    A   The games that made him fall in love with gaming.
    B   The competitive multi-player games.
    C   The games that are the most popular at the time.
    D   The games that can make him the most money.

Answers on pages 77–81

Put it to the test 2

You are going to read an extract from a blog post in which a health professional describes her job. For questions 31–36, read the text below and decide which answer fits best according to the text. For each question, mark the appropriate answer (A, B, C or D).

As a midwife, I have the honour of welcoming new life into the world on a daily basis. For those who may not know, a midwife is a health professional who specialises in supporting women when they are pregnant, as well as during and after childbirth.

Although I've always loved babies, I decided to go into this profession because I have always had a passion for helping others. After finishing high school, I considered going to medical college to become a doctor, but in the end I did a nursing degree. I then went on to specialise in midwifery, which I knew immediately was the right decision. It was the perfect fit for me because I wanted to work in a field where I could make a difference in people's lives, and being a midwife allows me to do just that.

It's not the best-paid job and my schedule depends on other people, but I wouldn't change it. The most amazing part of my job is being present for the birth of a baby.

There's nothing quite like the feeling of watching a new life enter the world, and I am honoured to be a part of that process. It's also incredibly satisfying to be able to provide support to new parents as they navigate the early days of parenthood.

Being a midwife, I love the relationships I build with my patients. It's not unusual for me to see the same women for several pregnancies, and it's always a joy to see how their families grow and change over time. Although I tend to be a bit hands-off after the birth, I still love being able to provide education and support to new mothers, and to see the confidence they gain as they become more comfortable in their roles as parents.

I've had the pleasure of attending a variety of births, from natural home births to hospital births with medical assistance. It's always a new experience to see the different ways women choose to give birth, and I've learned a lot from each experience. Last week alone I had one patient who was a professional athlete and continued running up until the day she gave birth, and another patient who came in to have one baby and left with twins!

However, in this line of work it's important to be able to think on your feet because things can change quickly during labour and delivery. It's crucial to be able to adapt to new situations as they come up. In the past, I've had to cancel birth plans and make quick decisions based on the safety of both mother and baby.

I remember one situation when I was attending a natural birth and the patient had turned down medication of any kind. Unfortunately, things started to change and, as the midwife, it was my responsibility to make a quick decision with the mother.

Even in those difficult moments, I know that I'm doing everything I can to give 100% to my patients. I realise that being a midwife is not for everyone, but for those who have a passion for it there's nothing else like it in the world. I feel incredibly lucky to be able to do what I do, and I know I will continue to find enjoyment in this career for as long as I do it. Despite how I feel, the job definitely has its challenges, like the emotions it produces in you and balancing work and personal life. For me, though, the rewards outweigh the challenges.

B2 Reading | Part 5: Multiple choice

31. What led to the author becoming a midwife?

- **A** She loved being around babies.
- **B** She wanted to help other people.
- **C** She worked as a doctor before specialising.
- **D** She felt inspired by what she experienced at nursing school.

32. In the third paragraph, the author explains that the best part of her job is

- **A** seeing a parent's reaction to their new baby.
- **B** the salary she is paid
- **C** the flexibility to work when she wants.
- **D** being there when the baby arrives.

33. What does the author say about her relationships with her patients?

- **A** She enjoys helping and informing new mothers.
- **B** She usually only sees patients for their first child.
- **C** She often sees new parents lose confidence.
- **D** She is very involved in the weeks after the baby arrives.

34. By attending a variety of births, the author has been

- **A** surprised that births often go more smoothly in a hospital setting.
- **B** interested to find out that births usually require hospital involvement.
- **C** surprised that births can be completely different for each person.
- **D** interested to learn that births are different if the mother is a very active person.

35. In line 25, 'think on your feet' means

- **A** to know how to deal with delivery issues safely.
- **B** to carefully follow the birth plan.
- **C** to be able to move around while working.
- **D** to react as necessary at the time.

36. In the final paragraph, what does the author say about her career?

- **A** She will be passionate about it for the remainder of her working life.
- **B** She thinks the hardest thing is hiding her emotions from patients.
- **C** She finds it difficult to give everything to her job, all of the time.
- **D** She feels that everyone would enjoy the job if they knew what it involved.

Answers on pages 81–85

Part 6: Gapped text

B2 First Reading

Prepare

This part of the B2 First Reading examination consists of a single page of text with six numbered gaps. These gaps represent missing sentences. After the text, there are seven sentences that are not in the right order. You have to read the text and the sentences, and decide which sentence best fits each gap. You will not need to use one of these sentences. There are 2 marks for each correct answer. This part checks your ability to:

- understand the structure and development of a text

- make thematic connections between the missing sentences and the text

- recognise connecting words that link the text and the missing sentences (these may include pronouns, like *he* or *she*, determiners like *this* or *these*, or linking words like *however* or *therefore*)

- recognise key words in the sentences before and after the gaps

- find linguistic evidence for your choice of answers.

Suggestions to help you do well in this task

- The text in this part is shorter than in Part 5, so if you have time you can skim-read just to get a general understanding – but this isn't essential!

- The most important thing to remember is that you **never** need to guess! There are always either 'grammatical' or 'contextual' clues to help you. What you need to do is read *extremely* carefully the sentences before and after each gap. These sentences will help you! They will contain grammar that you can match to the missing paragraph, e.g. pronouns, tenses, etc… If they don't match the option, then you know it is incorrect.

- The biggest mistake students make is to just read the text **before** the gap. By doing this, you might find a couple of options that fit grammatically, but it's the sentence that comes **after** the gap that often gives the context or uses contrast words that change the meaning and exclude an option that grammatically is okay.

- Once you've chosen your answer, re-read the text to double check that it makes sense As always, underline the grammatical and contextual links – if you can't do this then it's not the answer.

Have a go at some practice questions on the following pages.

Practise

You are going to read two extracts from a newspaper article about the television programme 'Who Wants to Be a Millionaire?'. Three sentences have been removed from the extract. Choose from sentences A–D the one that best fits each gap (1–3). There is one extra sentence that you do not need to use.

Extract 1

The TV quiz programme 'Who Wants to Be a Millionaire?' is essentially a knowledge-based game show that tests the intelligence, quick thinking and bravery of its contestants. **1** ☐ Contestants must choose the correct option to continue in the game and eventually try to win the top prize.

One of the show's most famous features is the system of lifelines, which provide contestants with assistance when they encounter challenging questions. **2** ☐ The 'Ask the Audience' lifeline allows contestants to rely on the combined knowledge of the studio audience, and '50:50' removes two incorrect answers, leaving the contestant with a 50% chance of choosing the correct option. These lifelines add an element of strategy to the game, as contestants must decide when and how to use them effectively.

The success of 'Who Wants to Be a Millionaire?' is due not only to its engaging gameplay but also in the charm of its hosts. Throughout the show's history, there have been many different hosts, each bringing their own unique style and personality. From the popular original host, Chris Tarrant, who was presenter of the UK version for 15 years, to the current UK host Jeremy Clarkson, each host has left their mark on the show. **3** ☐

The appeal of the huge prize has undoubtedly contributed to the show's appeal. Becoming a millionaire overnight is the dream of audiences around the world. The excitement builds as contestants progress through the questions, with each correct answer bringing them closer to the life-changing sum of money. The possibility of winning such a sum has made 'Who Wants to Be a Millionaire?' a fascinating experience for contestants and TV viewers alike.

A Their humour and ability to build excitement keep viewers on the edge of their seats, improving the overall experience of both TV and studio audiences.

B The first two of these are quite simple and are usually answered correctly by the contestants.

C The most well-known of these is 'Phone-a-Friend', which lets contestants call a chosen individual for help.

D This show consists of a series of multiple-choice questions of increasing difficulty, with a choice of four possible answers for each question.

Extract 2

An important factor that makes 'Who Wants to Be a Millionaire?' different is that is can be adapted to different cultures and languages. Including local celebrities and cultural references ensures that viewers will react to the show on a personal level. This strategy has contributed to the long life of the show as well as the global reach of the brand.

In addition to its television success, the show has expanded into other forms of media. **1** These adaptations provide an interactive experience in which players can test their knowledge and decision-making skills just like the show's contestants. The popularity of these games demonstrates the enduring appeal of 'Who Wants to Be a Millionaire?' beyond the television screen. Furthermore, the franchise's influence has even extended to the big screen with the world-famous film 'Slumdog Millionaire'. Directed by Danny Boyle, the movie tells the story of Jamal Malik, a young boy who appears on the Indian version of 'Who Wants to Be a Millionaire'. **2**

According to well-known psychologist Dr. Sarah Johnson, 'Who Wants to Be a Millionaire?' connects with our human brains in a way that makes it fascinating for both contestants and viewers. **3** This combination creates a powerful mixture of excitement and tension that causes the release of chemicals in the brain. The expectation of a potential million-pound prize stimulates the brain's reward system, making the experience highly enjoyable and turning viewers into addicts. This mix of intellectual challenge and decision-making keeps contestants on their toes and makes for absorbing television.

The worldwide impact of 'Who Wants to Be a Millionaire?' has been enormous. From its start as a television show, it has grown into a global sensation, fascinating audiences of all ages and backgrounds.

- **A** She explains that the way the show works brings together elements of knowledge-testing, decision-making under pressure and the appeal of a life-changing reward.
- **B** She manages to win the top prize by using her natural intelligence and ability to make quick decisions.
- **C** It has inspired board games and computer games, allowing fans to experience the excitement of the competition themselves.
- **D** The film explores the life experiences that help the youngster answer the quiz questions correctly.

Put it to the test 1

You are going to read an extract from a report that discusses the impact of Covid-19 on education. Six sentences have been removed. For questions 37–42, read the text below and, for each missing sentence, choose from options A–G the sentence that fits. There is one extra sentence that you do not need to use.

The impact of Covid-19 on education in the developing world

Online education isn't without its faults

The Covid-19 pandemic has had a huge impact on education worldwide, particularly in developing countries. **37** In this report, we will examine the impact of the pandemic on education in the developing world, with a focus on six specific countries.

At the beginning of the pandemic, many developing countries were forced to close schools and pause face-to-face learning. **38** Online education was not an option for many of these students due to a lack of internet access, computers and other necessary equipment.

In Nigeria, for example, a recent report by the United Nations Children's Fund (UNICEF) estimated that more than 10 million children are at risk of being left behind due to schools closing at the time. The report suggested that schools should have made alternative arrangements, such as radio or television broadcasts, to ensure that students did not fall behind in their studies.

39 According to a recent survey conducted by the National Education Association, 30% of Pakistani students did not attend online classes due to a lack of resources, while others struggled to keep up with the pace of online learning.

In Afghanistan the situation is even worse. Despite efforts in this country to build bridges between teachers and students through mobile phone-based learning, many students are still unable to access education due to a lack of devices and internet connectivity, as well as an unstable social and political situation.

40 In Bangladesh, for example, the government has provided free online education to students during the pandemic and has distributed radios and televisions to those who do not have internet access.

In Ethiopia, the government has also made suggestions to help students cope with the challenges of remote learning, including offering therapy services to students who are struggling to get over the mental health effects of the pandemic. Additionally, the government has been working with local organisations to provide students with books and other educational materials.

In Myanmar, where the pandemic has put the education of millions of children at risk, the government has been working to provide all students with access to online education. **41**

Despite these efforts, there is still much work to be done to ensure that students in developing countries are not left behind due to the pandemic. **42** They must also continue to explore alternative approaches to education and provide resources to help students get over the impact of the pandemic on their mental health and well-being.

So, while some countries have been able to adapt to online learning and provide alternative forms of education, others have struggled to keep up with the pace of change. Governments and organisations must continue to work together to find solutions to the challenges facing students in these countries, and ensure that they have the resources and support they need to continue their education.

24

B2 Reading | Part 6: Gapped text

A   Similarly, in Pakistan, where many students rely on public schools, the pandemic put children's education at risk.

B   It has been working with international organisations to provide devices and internet access to students who lack these resources.

C   While some of these countries were able to adapt quickly to online learning and remote teaching, others were not so lucky, leaving many students struggling to keep up with their studies.

D   With the help of these NGOs in the country, the government has managed to get a national news channel to broadcast educational programmes throughout the day, for different age groups and subjects.

E   However, despite these challenges, many developing countries have been working to make up for lost time and to find ways to help students catch up with their studies.

F   One major help would be for governments and organisations to take account of the unique challenges facing students in these countries and provide the necessary support to help them catch up with their studies.

G   This was a huge problem for a significant number of students who were already struggling to get by on limited resources.

Answers on pages 88–89

Put it to the test 2

You are going to read an extract from an article in which people discuss buying and selling shoes. Six sentences have been removed. For questions 37–42, read the text below and, for each missing sentence, choose from options A–G the sentence that fits. There is one extra sentence that you do not need to use.

Sneakerheads
The world of buying and selling sports shoes

The world of buying and selling sports shoes has become a crazy and highly profitable industry. **37** 'Sneakerheads', as they are often called, are people who collect and trade rare or limited-edition sneakers, and who are willing to pay a lot of money for the most unique pairs. Here, we will explore the ins and outs of the sneaker market and highlight a successful seller who has made a name for himself in this highly competitive industry.

To start with, the sneaker market has become a global phenomenon, with buyers and sellers all over the world. **38** Some even figure out ways to create unofficial versions of highly rare sneakers in order to buy up stock at lower prices and sell on at a significant profit. Sneakerheads are typically looking for rare or limited-edition sneakers, especially those with a unique design, history or connection to a well-known brand or artist. **39** Some examples of sneakers that sneakerheads might look out for include the Nike Air Jordan 1, Adidas Yeezy Boost and the Converse Chuck Taylor All-Star.

The most expensive sneakers can cost tens or even hundreds of thousands of dollars, depending on how difficult they are to find because of their design and history. For example, the Nike Mag sneakers worn by Michael J. Fox in the 1989 film 'Back to the Future Part II' sold for over $92,000 at a 2016 sale. In 2023, a pair of game-worn Nike Air Jordan sneakers sold for a record $2.2 million, making it the most expensive sneaker ever sold. **40**

One example of a successful sneaker trader is Benjamin Kickz, who is known as the 'Sneaker Don'. He started his business at the young age of 13 by buying and selling shoes online. He quickly made connections in the industry and started shopping around for rare and exclusive sneakers, prepared to pay huge amounts of money to get his hands on limited-edition pairs. **41** Benjamin Kickz later expanded into clothing and jewellery as well.

The sneaker industry is highly competitive and can be challenging, unless you have a reputation like Benjamin. **42** A well-timed phone call or message to their network of contacts can keep them informed and maintain their position as a top seller.

Therefore, the sneaker market is a place where anyone can get a piece of the action, but it requires hard work, commitment and a deep understanding of the industry. It's also helpful to build a network of like-minded people who you can buy and sell to, or simply have a discussion with about the rare and unique finds you're looking to get next.

A They may also be interested in old or classic sneakers that have become highly popular and searched for over time.

B It may sound like a job created for the social media crowd, but there's quite a bit of business knowledge required to be a successful sneakerhead.

C As his reputation grew, he started to make a name for himself among the celebrity crowd, with clients such as Drake, DJ Khaled and Chris Brown.

D In recent years, it has brought in a new word to describe people involved in the industry.

E It is worth noting, however, that most sneakerheads do not spend such high amounts on their collections, and there are many sneakers available at lower prices for those who are interested in the hobby.

F Many sneakerheads set up their own online stores or social media accounts to show their collections and attract potential buyers.

G Successful sellers like him know that they must bear in mind the latest trends and keep an eye on the market to stay ahead.

Answers on pages 89–91

Part 7: Multiple matching

B2 First Reading

Prepare

This part of the B2 First Reading examination consists of a series of questions followed by several short texts or a single text divided into paragraphs or sections. You have to match each question to a text or the section of a text in which you can find the information. There is 1 mark for each correct answer. Part 7 checks your ability to:

- skim a text for gist or general understanding
- read or scan a text for specific information
- notice textual clues while you scan
- understand the opinion and attitude of the writer
- locate detail in a large amount of text quickly.

Suggestions to help you do well in this task

- As this part is divided into four or five paragraphs, you need to treat this as a series of smaller reading-comprehension tasks. Don't panic about all the different texts! You first need to read the title and introduction to understand the context of each paragraph.

- As advised previously, **don't** read all of the paragraphs at once – you won't be able to remember everything! Instead, concentrate on just one of the paragraphs at a time.

- Read each paragraph carefully. Then start reading the questions, some of which will be easy to exclude quickly. If you think one could be the answer, start looking for synonyms used in the question and the paragraph and try to link them together.

- Each paragraph will have at least one question linked to it, but a paragraph may contain more than one question.

- As always, it's really important to underline *why* you think an answer is correct. When you have completed the first paragraph, repeat these steps for the others. Even if you have matched one question with a previous paragraph whilst completing the other paragraphs, just try to exclude it to double check that you have the right answer.

Have a go at some practice questions on the following pages.

Practise 1

You are going to read two texts about people who have worked in summer camps. For questions 1–6, read the texts on page 31 and choose the correct text (A or B).

Which person:

1		worked with teenagers?
2		worked with children with scientific interests?
3		mentions a weekly competition?
4		tried to develop children's ability to solve problems?
5		mentions that children's relatives saw what they had done?
6		encouraged children to work together in groups?

Text A – Mark Thompson (Sports Camp)

I had the pleasure of working as a monitor at a Sports Camp last summer. The camp was full of energy and excitement, with enthusiastic campers aged 8 to 12 who were passionate about various sports. My role as a monitor involved organising and managing sports activities such as football, basketball, swimming and tennis.

It was inspiring to see the campers' determination to improve their skills and their eagerness to take part in friendly competition. We also included activities to build teams and create a sense of friendship among the campers. Through these activities, they learned important values such as working as a team, determination and how to play sports fairly. One of the highlights of the camp was the sports tournament held at the end of each week. Campers eagerly prepared for this event, practising their chosen sport and making plans with members of their team.

It was incredible to see their hard work pay off as they showed their abilities and celebrated each other's achievements. The Sports Camp was not only about sports; we also organised fun leisure activities to give campers a varied experience. From talent shows to treasure hunts, we encouraged their creativity and developed a sense of fun and community.

Text B – Emily Eastwood (STEM Camp)

Hi. My name is Emily, and I had an amazing time working as a teacher at a STEM Camp last summer. The camp was designed for curious minds between the ages of 12 and 15 who were enthusiastic about science, technology, engineering and maths.

At the STEM Camp, we tried to make learning fun and interactive. I had the pleasure of guiding the campers through a variety of hands-on experiments and projects. From building and programming robots to conducting chemistry experiments, every day was a new opportunity for the campers to explore and discover the wonders of STEM. One of the highlights of the camp was the science fair, where the campers demonstrated their individual projects to other children and their parents.

It was truly inspiring to see their creativity and determination. The atmosphere was full of excitement and curiosity as everyone exchanged ideas and learned from one another. As a teacher, my role extended beyond the classroom. I encouraged critical thinking and problem-solving skills in the campers by organising team challenges and group discussions. It was incredible to see their enthusiasm and watch them develop a deep passion for STEM subjects.

Practise 2

You are going to read two more texts about people who have worked in summer camps. For questions 1–6, read the texts on page 33 and choose the correct text (A or B).

Which person:

1. [ ] describes how the children felt proud of what they achieved?
2. [ ] mentions that children made something unusual for people to wear?
3. [ ] describes a camp situated in a wooded area?
4. [ ] describes activities that encouraged children to work together?
5. [ ] describes how the children became more confident due to their experience?
6. [ ] mentions that their group camped at night?

Text A – Lee Kass (Adventure Camp)

I worked as a teacher at an Adventure Camp last summer. The camp was located in the middle of a picturesque forest, surrounded by tall trees and clean lakes. Our campers were between 8 and 12 years old, and their enthusiasm for outdoor activities was catching! Each day at camp was filled with thrilling adventures. We went walking and rock climbing, and tried a variety of other sports. As a teacher, I was responsible for leading educational sessions that linked to the camp's activities. It was so rewarding to see the campers' curiosity and eagerness to learn. We explored the natural environment and conducted science experiments outdoors.

One of the most memorable experiences was the overnight camping trip. We set up tents near a sparkling river and spent the evening sharing stories and cooking food on the campfire. The sense of friendship among the campers was truly wonderful.

Overall, working as a teacher at the Adventure Camp was an incredible experience. Seeing the campers develop new skills and make lasting friendships was very rewarding. It was a summer filled with laughter, learning and unforgettable adventures.

Text B – Alex Rodriguez (Arts & Crafts Camp)

Hello, everyone! My name is Alex, and I had a wonderful time working at an Arts and Crafts Camp last summer. The camp was the perfect place for creative children between the ages of 6 and 10 who were passionate about expressing themselves through various artistic ways. At the Arts and Crafts Camp, we began exciting new artistic journeys every day. From painting and making sculptures to creating unique jewellery, the campers had the opportunity to explore their creativity and discover their artistic talents. As a teacher, I provided guidance and encouragement, helping the children to be imaginative and develop their artistic skills.

One of the highlights of the camp was the art exhibition, where the campers proudly displayed their creations to their families and friends. You could see the sense of achievement and pride that showed through their smiles as they explained the stories behind their artworks.

In addition to the creative activities, the Arts and Crafts Camp also encouraged personal growth. We organised storytelling sessions, where campers had the chance to share their own stories and take part in imaginative play. This allowed them to develop their communication skills and increase their confidence. We also organised art projects that required cooperation and the children to work in teams. Campers worked together to create large paintings and sculptures that created a sense of community and among them.

Put it to the test 1

You are going to read a newspaper article about volunteering for charity organisations. For questions 43–52, read the text below and, on page 35, choose the correct paragraph (A–D).

Give time, not money
Four people talk about supporting charities by volunteering

A. Kiran: Being a volunteer at the shelter – a place where people without a home can stay – has given me the chance to get together with, and get to know, people from all walks of life. We spend hours together, and I've formed some fantastic relationships with the visitors. I try to cheer them up, make them laugh and warm them up with kind words. It's amazing to see the change in them from when they first arrive, and it makes me feel like I'm making a difference. We don't just hand out food and go our separate ways. We have a bit of a laugh, talk about our lives and share our experiences. It's essential to treat everyone with kindness and respect, whatever their circumstances. Seeing the visitors smile and laugh, even for a moment, is incredibly rewarding. I'm grateful for the opportunity to volunteer at the shelter, and I hope to continue doing so for a long time to come.

B. Elisabeth: As a charity shop worker, I volunteer two afternoons per week to help out in any way I can. It's a great way to keep busy now that I'm retired, and I love being able to give back to the community in this way. When I'm at the shop, I spend my time organising and displaying items; helping customers shop around for the perfect thing. It's always interesting to see the variety of items that come into the shop that can now be sold for much less – from vintage clothing and unique home decoration to practical kitchen devices and children's toys. I suppose some customers buy items to do them up and then sell them on, but it's also exciting to find hidden gems that are perfect for my own home or wardrobe. Finally, I started volunteering to fill my time, but after that, I realised how practical and rewarding it is to be a part of this charity's mission.

C. Ivan: Taking a year out from university to come here to Syria and take part in volunteer work has been one of the most meaningful experiences of my life. Although there have been some very scary moments due to the conflict in the country, I know that I am making a difference and am helping those who have been affected by it. Every day, I work side-by-side with other volunteers and local aid workers to put up shelters, distribute food and supplies, and provide work training to those who have been affected by the conflict. It's humbling to see how much these simple acts of kindness can mean to those who are struggling to survive in such difficult circumstances. There have been moments when I have witnessed the courage of seriously ill patients or the commitment of brave colleagues, which reminds me to be grateful for the simple things I have in my life.

D. Carlos: Being a volunteer for The Samaritans is one of the best things I've ever done. I spend time answering the phone, ready to take calls from anyone who needs someone to talk to. The ability to listen patiently is key, and it's important to make sure that the caller feels heard and understood. Sometimes, all it takes is a kind word or someone to listen to help a person take back control of their life. Nowadays, with the world being so fast-moving and stressful, it's easy for people to feel lonely and that nobody understands what they're going through. By being sympathetic and listening, we can help make a difference in someone's life. It can be challenging at times, but I know that if I stick it out and keep doing what I'm doing, I can make a real impact on the people who call us in need.

B2 Reading | Part 7: Multiple matching

Which person:

43 ☐ mentions that they work somewhere that sells used items at a discount?

44 ☐ believes that helping those who have been affected by social or political violence is very satisfying?

45 ☐ describes how volunteering allows them to meet people from different backgrounds?

46 ☐ finds that volunteering is a great way to spend time now that they've finished work?

47 ☐ states that their listening skills are crucial for their volunteering work?

48 ☐ says that they're always curious about the range of things that end up at their charity shop?

49 ☐ suggests that the speed of modern life can make people feel alone?

50 ☐ thinks that they have learned to appreciate everything they have because of their volunteer work?

51 ☐ explains that they will return to their studies after their volunteer work?

52 ☐ says that it's important not to judge those that need help?

Answers on pages 93–94

Put it to the test 2

You are going to read a newspaper article about whether people prefer cats or dogs. Six sentences have been removed. For questions 43–52, read the text below and, on page 37, choose the correct paragraph (A–D).

Cats or dogs?
Four people talk about their pet preference

A. Laura: As someone who prefers cats to dogs, I've always found it annoying how dogs can be so needy. They're always wanting attention, and when they don't get it they'll bark and let you know. When I'm around dogs, I feel like I have to constantly run after them to make sure they're not getting into trouble or bothering other people. To me, dogs can do more harm than good, especially if they're not taught properly. On the other hand, I respect cats for their independence. They don't need constant attention or approval from their owners. They're content to curl up in a cosy spot and mind their own business. Sure, they may run away when they're not in the mood for socialising, but that's just part of their charm. Dogs, meanwhile, will do anything for a treat or to please their owners, but then they're right back to being needy again. For me, the choice is clear: cats are just better than dogs.

B. Marie: I always say: 'love me, love my dogs'. I can't imagine my life without them. They're my constant companions; always eager to back up my every move and wag their tail at the slightest sign of affection. I have a pack of dogs that I get along with so well – we go out together all the time. They're more than just animals to me – they're my family. One of the best things about having dogs is that they're the perfect excuse for a good walk. My dogs keep me fit and active, and I love exploring new trails and parks with them. Additionally, I absolutely love dressing them up in little costumes. It's enjoyable for me to see how nice they look and how much attention they get from people. But, at the end of the day, it's not about how my dogs *look*, it's about how they make me *feel*.

C. Carmen: On the one hand, I can appreciate that cats have their charms. But, they're just not as awesome as dogs. For me, cats are so arrogant. They'll sit on the arm of the sofa and look down at you like they're judging your every move. Dogs, on the other hand, just want to carry on and have fun with you. Secondly, let's talk about energy levels. Good luck trying to get a cat to fetch something or go for a run. Dogs will play until they get tired, and then they'll still want to go for a walk. They're well said to be man's best friend for a reason. And, let's not forget, dogs will do anything for a snack whereas I think a cat would eat *you* if they could. So, I would say the choice is pretty clear: dogs all the way!

D. Stephanie: I've been unsure about having a pet, but if I were to get one, I think I would go for a cat. I don't have any pets at the moment, but if I did I would almost definitely have a cat. They're independent creatures, and I don't think I have the energy for a dog. Plus, they're known to be cleaner than dogs, which is a definite plus for me. Of course, there are some things to consider before making the final decision. Cats can be quite independent and aren't so keen on affection, whereas dogs are known for their love and loyalty. However, I think I could live with that. Actually, the more I think about it, the more I'm convinced that a cat is the right choice for me. Now, the only thing left to do is to find the perfect one.

B2 Reading | Part 7: Multiple matching

Which person:

43	explains that cats have bad attitudes?
44	thinks that it's nice when a cat doesn't demand affection?
45	mentions that they have several pets?
46	believes that despite the attention of strangers, their pets' appearance isn't important?
47	suggests that looking after a dog would take up more time than a cat?
48	states that cats demand much less attention than dogs?
49	sounds as though they're trying to justify the idea of getting a pet?
50	finds that training a pet is essential to avoid trouble?
51	believes that cats are less energetic than dogs?
52	explains that their pets help them to stay healthy?

Answers on pages 94–95

Practice tests

Test 1 | pages 41–48

Part 5: A Journey of Self-Discovery   *42*
Part 6: The Modern Face of Chess   *44*
Part 7: Earning a living as a musician   *46*

Test 2 | pages 49–56

Part 5: Hay Fever   *50*
Part 6: Extreme Marathon Running   *52*
Part 7: Generation X versus Generation Z   *54*

Test 3 | pages 57–64

Part 5: Tomato Growing   *58*
Part 6: The Joy of Bird Watching   *60*
Part 7: *The Parent* by Fabio Astrella   *62*

Test 4 | pages 65–72

Part 5: Trends in Urban Planning   *66*
Part 6: The Rise and Evolution of Women's Football   *68*
Part 7: The Pitfalls of Wish Cycling   *70*

Cambridge B2 First Reading

Practice test 1

Part 5

You are going to read an extract from an article about making a journey on foot. For questions **31–36**, read the text below and decide which answer (**A, B, C or D**) fits best.

A Journey of Self-Discovery

Deciding to take the challenge of walking El Camino de Santiago can be a life-changing experience for anyone. This ancient trail is a network of ways which lead to the cathedral of Santiago de Compostela in Galicia in Northwest Spain, where the remains of the apostle Saint James The Great are kept. Pilgrims, people who make the journey as an act of religious devotion, come from many different backgrounds and seek the transformative power of this famous path. Pope Alexander VI declared El Camino de Santiago one of the three great pilgrimages in Christendom. So, what are the motivations and experiences of the pilgrims who take on the challenge of walking El Camino de Santiago?

María, an enthusiastic traveller with a strong desire for adventure, wanted to connect with nature, find spiritual enlightenment, and test her physical and mental limits. The stories of self-discovery and the beauty of the path had fascinated her for years, and she finally felt ready to set off on the pilgrimage. "As soon as I began my journey," she says, "I quickly realised that the trail demanded my determination and ability to recover quickly. The hilly terrain, constantly sloping up and down along the path, tested my endurance, and the ever-changing weather required me to adapt."

María faced challenges like blisters on her feet, tired muscles and moments of exhaustion along the way. However, she discovered a strength within herself that she didn't know existed, pushing her beyond what she previously thought her limits were.

Despite the physical challenges, María found peace in the simple life on the trail. She says, "Each day was filled with walking on the ancient cobblestones, enjoying the stunning views of the Spanish countryside and forming connections with fellow pilgrims from around the world. People were an incredible variety of ages, nationalities and backgrounds, and everyone walking the trail seemed to feel a sense of shared purpose." María had serious conversations with these diverse individuals, gaining new perspectives and understanding of people on a deeper level.

The journey also provided María with time for self-reflection. She had moments to think about her life, her beliefs and her place in the world. "Walking the Camino allowed me to disconnect from the noise of daily life and focus on my inner thoughts and emotions. This introspection has helped me gain valuable insights into myself and my values."

One of the most enjoyable aspects of the pilgrimage for María was the breath-taking natural scenery. The beauty of the Spanish countryside, with its rolling hills, valleys and charming villages, left her in awe. Each new day brought fresh landscapes to explore and appreciate.

Now that it's over, María has taken some time to reflect on her trip. "Looking back on my journey, I realise that there are a few things that I might do differently if I were to organise it again. Firstly, I'd pay more attention to physical preparation, ensuring I was adequately fit and equipped for the long walks. Then I would plan the daily distances more carefully to avoid overdoing it. Finally, I'd spend more time interacting with the locals and immersing myself in the culture of the regions I passed through."

We mentioned earlier that walking El Camino de Santiago can be a transformative experience. María's motivations to seek nature, spirituality and personal challenges were definitely satisfied throughout her journey. But what were her thoughts after actually completing the Way?

Maria said: "I discovered an inner strength that showed me how much I could push myself to keep going. However, I had not considered how much my general fitness would benefit from doing such a physically demanding journey. I feel healthier physically, as well as spiritually." Maria also formed deep connections with fellow pilgrims. "I met people who I will always remember. I'm not sure I will ever meet them again, but I will always value the time we spent together. The simplicity of life on the trail allowed me to reflect on myself and appreciate the beauty of life. I will always keep my experiences in my memory and in my heart. It is an incredible experience I would recommend to anyone."

31 How does the writer describe the people who make this journey?

   A They are all experienced walkers.
   B They have the same motivation as each other.
   C They have a variety of life experiences.
   D They hope the journey will improve their lives.

32 How does Maria explain her decision to make this particular journey?

   A She had heard other travellers' accounts of making the journey.
   B She was determined to prove she was physically capable of walking that distance.
   C She knew she would find the landscape along the route interesting.
   D She had always been keen on adventures of this kind.

33 What did Maria appreciate most about taking part in this walk?

   A The peaceful atmosphere along the route.
   B Meeting people from many different countries.
   C Meeting people who were very different from herself.
   D Making meaningful contact with so many different people.

34 In paragraph 5, what does Maria mean by the phrase 'the noise of daily life'?

   A The sounds associated with her normal home life.
   B Everything she has to think about during her home life.
   C The sounds that surround people living in towns and cities.
   D Difficulties and challenges she has to face in her normal life.

35 If Maria repeated the experience, what would she do differently while on the walk?

   A walk longer distances each day
   B attend more events of cultural interest
   C make more contact with people in the areas the route went through
   D take more equipment with her

36 Looking back on her journey, what does Maria find surprising?

   A That she made such good friendships with fellow travellers.
   B That the walk had improved her physical condition.
   C That life on the walk was so simple.
   D That doing the walk would be so hard physically.

Part 6

You are going to read an article about the increasing popularity of chess. Six sentences have been removed from the article. Choose from sentences **A–G** the one that fits each gap (**37–43**). There is one sentence you do not need to use.

The Modern Face of Chess:
A Game Transformed by Technology and Popularity

Chess, often called 'the game of kings', has a rich history, originating in ancient India before developing and spreading to different countries where it gained popularity among the elite. Eventually it became popular throughout the world.

Throughout history, chess has been more than simply a game. **37**　　 From the royal courts of medieval Europe to the coffeehouses of the 17th and 18th centuries, chess has entertained players and spectators alike. However, in recent years, chess has experienced a renaissance, capturing the attention of new generations and reaching never-before-seen levels of popularity. **38**　　 This development has transformed the way chess is played and enjoyed. Online platforms and mobile applications have brought the game to the fingertips of millions, providing opportunities for players of all levels to compete. Platforms like chess.com and lichess.org offer a wide range of features, including virtual tournaments, interactive tutorials and the ability to connect with other players and fans from around the world. **39**　　

Moreover, technology has enabled the emergence of chess engines and artificial intelligence (AI) analysis, revolutionising the way players study and prepare for games. **40**　　 These AI-powered tools have become valuable resources for both amateurs and professionals, pushing the limits of chess knowledge and enabling players to reach new heights of understanding.

Another significant reason behind the increasing popularisation of chess is the influence of television programmes and streaming platforms. **41**　　 The Netflix mini-series 'The Queen's Gambit', with its fascinating storyline, has excited viewers and showcased the intellectual demands of the game. This series started a renewed interest in chess, and inspired a new wave of enthusiasts to start playing. Streaming platforms like YouTube have also played an important role in making chess accessible and entertaining for a broader audience. Grandmasters and skilled players now regularly livestream their matches, providing useful commentary and communicating with viewers. **42**　　 The popularity of chess streamers has increased dramatically, drawing millions of viewers and making chess a spectator sport in its own right.

The combination of technology and media exposure has not only attracted new players to the game but has also expanded the player base. Chess, once considered an exclusive activity for intellectuals, is now accessible to anyone with an internet connection and a desire to learn. This inclusivity has allowed individuals of all ages and from all backgrounds to participate in the game and experience its unique challenges.

A In recent years, chess has found its way onto the small screen, captivating audiences with thrilling matches and colourful personalities.

B It has been a battleground for strategic minds, a symbol of intellectual ability and a test of quick thinking.

C Much of this new interest is due to the arrival of new technology and the rise of media platforms.

D The film was also a massive success with the majority of the critics who reviewed it.

E These platforms have created a global chess community, where players can learn from grandmasters, analyse games and participate in friendly competitions.

F This interactive feature has created a sense of community and camaraderie, with viewers participating in chat discussions and cheering for their favourite players.

G With powerful chess engines like Stockfish, players can analyse their moves, spot mistakes and explore alternative strategies.

Part 7

You are going to read about the lives of four professional musicians. For questions **43–52**, choose from the sections (**A–D**). The sections may be chosen more than once.

Which musician:

43	says they sometimes have to play at times they would rather spend with friends and family?
44	finds it difficult to make enough money from playing music?
45	enjoys playing with other musicians, but finds it limiting?
46	receives some of their income from audience members who appreciate their music?
47	plays music on celebratory occasions?
48	feels discouraged by the challenges they face?
49	says their pattern of work allows them time to get better at playing music?
50	finds it very difficult to find enough opportunities to play?
51	says they have no choice about what and how they play?
52	enjoys playing in a range of very different venues?

Earning a living as a musician

Four people talk about their profession

A. Being a musician is my passion: I eat, breathe and live music. However, the reality of trying to earn a living from music has been incredibly challenging. The journey of a struggling musician is filled with highs and lows, and I find myself constantly questioning my choices. Financially, it's been tough. There are few opportunities for gigs, and the competition is fierce. It feels like a never-ending battle to secure paying gigs, and even when I do, the compensation is often poor. It's depressing to put my heart into my music only to struggle to make ends meet. Emotionally, the constant uncertainty has an effect. I'm always experiencing self-doubt and I wonder if my talent will ever get noticed. But, despite these difficulties, there are still moments of pure joy. When I'm playing my music to a small audience that genuinely appreciates what I do, it's a real high.

B. As a guitarist playing in flamenco venues in Madrid, I've found a niche that allows me to earn a good living. It's an incredible feeling to have found success doing what I love. The 'tablaos' are bustling with tourists, and the demand for live music is always high. Financially, I'm finally stable. The tablaos pay well, and tips from enthusiastic tourists can be generous. It's rewarding to see my talent being appreciated and rewarded, allowing me to support myself comfortably. These shows provide a regular schedule that allows me to focus on my craft and continue improving. However, there are some negative things. Playing at the tablaos can be repetitive, doing the same thing night after night. Sometimes I feel my creativity is being limited. While the money is good, I miss the artistic freedom that comes with making my own music.

C. Being a musician in an orchestra has its perks, but also comes with frustrations that weigh heavily on my soul. I have a regular income, which is a rare thing in the music industry. However, the trade-off is a lack of creative freedom. Playing in an orchestra means sticking to strict musical interpretations and following a conductor's lead. While this provides a sense of playing together as a unit and discipline, it often feels like my artistic voice is not heard. I really want to explore my own musical ideas. Additionally, the repetitive nature of playing the same repertoire again and again can become monotonous. The excitement I once felt performing in a famous orchestra has become lessened. However, there are still moments I love. When the entire orchestra comes together, creating a captivating symphony, it's a wonderful experience. Those moments remind me why I originally fell in love with music.

D. Being a wedding singer is an absolute joy. It's an honour to be a part of people's special day and bring them happiness. I genuinely love my job, and I think it shows in my performances. Financially, wedding gigs provide a reliable source of income. There are many highs to being a wedding singer; witnessing the love and joy on the faces of the happy couple and their guests as I play for them is truly rewarding. Moreover, the variety of wedding themes and musical styles keeps my work exciting. From small garden ceremonies to receptions in massive houses or hotels, each event brings its own unique atmosphere and musical demands. Of course, there are also some lows. Performing at weddings means working on weekends and holidays, giving up personal time with my loved ones. It can be physically demanding, with long hours of rehearsals and different sets of music to perform.

Cambridge B2 First Reading

Practice test 2

Part 5

You are going to read an article about a common complaint suffered by some people during summer months. For questions **31–36**, read the text below and decide which answer (**A, B, C or D**) fits best.

Hay Fever

Hay fever, also known as allergic rhinitis, is a common problem that affects many people, especially during spring and summer. These allergies happen when our body reacts strongly to things it comes into contact with, such as pollen, dust mites or pet fur in the air. This can cause annoying symptoms like sneezing a lot, having a runny or stuffy nose, itchy eyes and an irritated throat.

Hay fever is increasingly common in many places, and there are a few reasons for this. One reason is the changing climate, which leads to longer pollen seasons. This means more pollen in the air, which makes hay fever worse. Another reason is that cities have fewer green spaces but more plants that cause allergies, such as ragweed (a plant that you've probably never noticed). Pollution in cities can also make hay fever worse. Additionally, changes in hygiene and less contact with certain germs, to which our bodies would have built up a natural defence in the past, might increase the chances of developing hay fever.

This annoying and often painful condition can really get in the way of enjoying life, but there are ways to manage it and feel better.

The main cause of hay fever is that our immune system, the body's natural defence to disease, over-reacts to harmless things around us. When we come into contact with allergens, our immune system releases substances called antibodies that make us feel awful. One common symptom is non-stop sneezing. It's like we can't control our sneezes and need to keep grabbing tissues to wipe our noses. It can be really distracting and make it hard to focus on work or studying.

Another annoying symptom is having a runny or blocked nose. It feels like we can't breathe properly because our nose gets swollen and makes a lot of mucus. Blowing our nose all the time becomes a regular thing. Sometimes, a blocked nose can even give us headaches and make our sinuses hurt.

Hay fever also makes our eyes feel itchy and watery. They can become red and sore, and can become super sensitive to light. It's hard to resist the need to rub them, but that usually makes things worse and could even cause eye infections. Wearing sunglasses or using special eye drops can help protect our eyes and make them feel better.

On top of all that, hay fever can give us a sore throat. It feels uncomfortable and makes us cough because our throat gets irritated by the allergens floating around. Talking or swallowing can become difficult when our throat is particularly sensitive.

Thankfully, there are ways to manage hay fever and make the symptoms more bearable. One thing that we can try to do is avoid the things that cause our allergies, but it's not always easy, especially when there's pollen in the air. Taking medicine such as antihistamine, which can be purchased without a doctor's prescription, can help by stopping the substances that make us feel bad. We can also use nasal sprays or eye drops to reduce inflammation and help us feel better.

If our hay fever is severe and doesn't get better with over-the-counter treatments, it's a good idea to see a doctor. They might give you a prescription for stronger medicines or suggest immunotherapy, which is a long-term treatment that helps our body become less sensitive to allergens.

In addition to medicine, there are practical things we can do to minimise our contact with allergens. Keeping windows closed, using air purifiers to clean the air and regularly cleaning our living spaces can help reduce allergens in the air. Wearing hats outside can also protect us from pollen. It's a good idea to check the pollen levels each day and plan our outdoor activities when they're lower. This information is sometimes included in weather forecasts.

Hay fever can be a real nuisance, but with the right treatment and self-care we can find relief from the symptoms. It's important to talk to a doctor to get proper advice. By taking steps to avoid allergens and using the right medicines, we can take control of our lives and still enjoy being outdoors, even when hay fever tries to spoil our fun.

31 How does climate change affect hay fever?

   A It makes the situation in towns and cities worse.
   B It leads to increased levels of pollution.
   C It affects the length of time when pollen levels are high.
   D It increases the number of germs in the atmosphere.

32 Why do hay fever sufferers react badly to things that should not cause them any harm?

   A Their bodies respond more strongly than they should.
   B Their bodies have a weakened defence system.
   C Their bodies have no natural defences.
   D Their bodies cannot produce substances that would protect them.

33 Why are hay fever sufferers advised to wear sunglasses?

   A Wearing sunglasses can prevent their eyes from watering.
   B Hay fever can make their eyes react more than normal to light.
   C Wearing sunglasses can prevent eye infections.
   D To prevent them from rubbing their eyes.

34 Why does the writer suggest hay fever sufferers try using sprays and drops?

   A They do not need to be prescribed by a doctor.
   B They can stop the allergic reaction to harmful substances.
   C They can stop sufferers from sneezing.
   D They can make their eyes and nose less painful.

35 Why might hay fever sufferers decide to see a doctor?

   A If they are particularly worried about their situation.
   B If their condition is not improved by medicines that can be bought easily.
   C If their condition is taking a long time to improve.
   D if they need to be treated over a longer period of time.

36 Why might hay fever sufferers pay attention to weather forecasts?

   A Some forecasts broadcast information about pollen levels.
   B To help them decide where to spend their time.
   C Because weather conditions can affect how hay fever sufferers feel.
   D To help them plan their day.

Part 6

You are going to read an article about a marathon runner. Six sentences have been removed from the article. Choose from sentences **A–G** the one that fits each gap (**37–43**). There is one sentence you do not need to use.

No Limits:
Journalist Simon Stone meets an Extreme Marathon Runner

John Davis is an extraordinary individual in the world of extreme marathon running. He has become a household name thanks to the reality TV show that followed him recently. Known for pushing his physical and mental limits, John has tackled some of the most challenging races on the planet. Let's explore his motivations and experiences and try to get a better understanding of this man.

"I've always been fascinated by pushing limits and discovering what lies beyond the limits of comfort," John explained when I asked him what got him started in Extreme Marathon running. **37** The thrill of completing that race started a desire within me to explore further."

Extreme marathons often involve running through difficult and dangerous terrains and enduring unpleasant conditions. I asked John what drives him to participate in those incredibly challenging races. **38** "I believe that by pushing myself to the edge, I can surprise myself by how strong I can be."

I asked John if he could share an example of an extreme marathon that left a lasting impression on him. **39** This was held in the deserts of Namibia where temperatures rose to more than 40 degrees Celsius. "The enormous sand dunes seemed never-ending, and dehydration became a real threat. **40** Crossing the finish line was an experience I'll remember forever."

The mental strength required for such races must be huge. **41** He replied: "Mental strength is undoubtedly crucial. When exhaustion sets in and doubt begins to enter my mind, I remind myself of the purpose behind my running. I visualise my loved ones cheering me on, and I draw strength from knowing that I am capable of overcoming any obstacle."

Extreme marathon running involves risks and potential injuries. I wanted to know how John reduces the risk of these dangers and ensures his safety. "Safety is the most important thing in extreme marathon running. **42** I also equip myself with the correct gear and supplies, such as a reliable GPS device, protective clothing and the necessary hydration and nutrition.

"To all those who dream of succeeding, I say: believe in yourself. Extreme marathon running is not just about the physical aspect; it's a mental and emotional journey. Be prepared to face difficulties, adapt to them and enjoy the victories, no matter how small they are. Remember, it's not always about winning but rather the personal growth you achieve along the way.

A He told me that one of the most memorable races he had participated in was the 'Desert Storm Ultra'.

B I asked John how he stayed motivated during the long and demanding hours on the course.

C John's amazing determination, mental strength and love for the challenge have taken him on incredible journeys.

D Apparently, It had all begun a few years earlier when he decided to challenge himself by running his first marathon.

E Before each race, I research the course, understand the potential dangers involved and do lots of physical training.

F However, the sense of community among the runners and a complete determination to overcome these dangers fuelled my spirit.

G "For me, extreme marathons are more than just physical challenges; they're a journey of self-discovery and personal growth," he said.

Part 7

You are going to read what four people say about modern generations. For questions **43–52**, choose from the sections (**A–D**). The sections may be chosen more than once.

Which person says:

43		Generation X has had to learn a lot about digital technology in a short time?
44		they lived through a time when the economy was unpredictable?
45		they were educated in a rather old-fashioned way?
46		their work depends on their ability to understand how shoppers think and act?
47		they appreciate having grown up in a technologically advanced world?
48		that members of the other generation are capable of doing many things simultaneously?
49		that Generation X is able to make links between digital technology and older ways of working?
50		that their generation understands the need to plan for the future?
51		the fact that their generation is both imaginative and technically capable makes them different?
52		Generation X has had to get used to the idea that business can be done digitally?

Generation X versus Generation Z

Four people talk about their generation

A. As a member of Generation X, I have witnessed huge technological changes in the field of education. Growing up, we had limited access to information compared to today's Generation Z. We relied on traditional teaching methods, developing critical thinking, face-to-face communication and an appreciation of books. Our ability to adapt to new technologies made us creative and adaptable learners. In comparison, Generation Z has grown up with a wealth of digital resources and instant access to information. As digital natives, they effortlessly navigate complex systems, displaying remarkable multi-tasking abilities and exceptional digital skills. However, despite their technological ability, I believe that our generation's advantage lies in our ability to solve problems creatively. Our experience of learning without the help of instant answers and our experience of diverse perspectives have created a unique skill set. We have a depth of knowledge that comes from processing and collecting information from various sources.

B. I belong to Generation Z, and am grateful for the technological developments that have shaped our lives. We are the generation known for our digital fluency, having grown up surrounded by technology. The world of digital tools, social media and online connectivity is our natural environment. By contrast, Generation X had to adapt to the rapid changes brought about by new technology. They possess valuable experience and a strong work ethic, but their learning curve for digital tools has been very steep. Our generation's intuitive understanding of technology gives us a natural advantage in fields that require innovation. With this strength, Generation Z brings a fresh perspective to industries that demand technological know-how. Our ability to adapt quickly to emerging trends gives us a strong position in today's tech-driven world. However, we recognise the strengths of Generation X with their valuable insights that bridge the gap between traditional methods and digital innovation.

C. I was born in 1975, so, as a member of Generation X working in the finance industry, I know the unique strengths we bring to the table. We grew up during a time of economic instability. Through our years of experience, we have developed a keen understanding of risk management, long-term planning and the importance of saving for the future. Generation Z, on the other hand, has grown up in a more financially inter-connected world. They are comfortable with digital financial tools and easily navigate online banking and investment platforms. Their fresh perspective and digital literacy are important in the fast-paced world of finance. However, our years of experience and deep understanding of financial systems give us a solid foundation to navigate uncertain economic landscapes. Generation X has lived through ups and downs in the market and economic downturns, which has enabled us to rely on our knowledge and experience to make informed decisions.

D. As a young person working in the marketing industry, I have a unique set of skills and perspectives. Our generation, Gen Z, has grown up in an era of social media and digital marketing, giving us a natural understanding of online platforms and consumer behaviour. We have perfected our skills in creating engaging content and persuading social media influencers to deliver precisely targeted marketing campaigns. Our ability to use creativity with technology equally well sets us apart. By contrast, Generation X has had to adapt to the rise of digital marketing. Their strengths lie in traditional strategies, which are valued by certain industries. However, our generation's ability to navigate the changing digital world and exploit the power of social media enables us to create innovative and visually attractive content that appeals to our peers. We have an ability to analyse social media trends and use emerging platforms to reach target audiences effectively.

Cambridge B2 First Reading

Practice test 3

Part 5

You are going to read an article that gives advice about growing tomatoes. For questions **31–36**, read the text below and decide which answer (**A, B, C or D**) fits best.

Tomato Growing

Growing tomatoes can be a beneficial and satisfying activity, whether you have an enormous garden, a cosy greenhouse or limited space. To help you grow tomatoes successfully, here's some valuable advice related to a variety of growing conditions.

Firstly, make sure that, right from planting your tomato seeds, you create a suitable environment. Tomatoes love warmth and sunlight, so place them in a location that receives plenty of natural light. If you're growing them indoors, think about using grow lights to supplement the natural light they receive. Keep them away from cold air and sudden temperature changes. Remember, a cosy, sunny spot will make your tomato plants feel at home.

Transferring your tomato seedlings into larger containers or the garden is a very important part of the process. Wait until the seedlings have developed a couple of sets of true leaves before transplanting them. Handle them gently, avoiding any damage to the delicate stems and roots. Remember, plants feel shock when they are transplanted, so be gentle and give your seedlings time to adjust to their new home.

For those lucky enough to have a garden, start by selecting the right location for your plants. Choose a spot that receives lots of sunlight and has soil where rainwater will not collect and drown your plants. If you plant them in a shady corner, they might disappoint you with a small crop due to the lack of light.

Prepare the soil by enriching it with compost – the decaying remains of other plants, or manure (the natural droppings of animals) – which will provide your tomato plants with the nutrients they need to become strong and healthy. Don't be afraid to get your hands dirty and dig deep. Remember, you get out what you put in, so invest your time in good soil preparation.

When being watered, tomatoes need a delicate balance; avoid drowning them with too much water or leaving them too dry. Water them deeply but not too often, allowing the soil to dry out slightly between waterings. Remember, it's better for them to be thirsty than to drown.

The main advantage of using a greenhouse is a significant extension of the tomato-growing season. In addition to this, the glass or plastic walls of a greenhouse protect plants from bad weather conditions. Ensure proper ventilation in the greenhouse to prevent your tomato plants from feeling like they're in a pressure cooker. Remember, fresh air is most important in a greenhouse.

Consider using wooden sticks to support your tomato plants and keep them from spreading all over the place like wild weeds. This will help the air to flow and prevent disease. Remember, a little support goes a long way.

Now, what if you have very limited space? Don't worry! Even with a small balcony or patio, you can still enjoy tomatoes grown at home. Select plants that will not grow large fruits because these are not suitable for container gardening. Get creative with hanging baskets, vertical gardens or even re-purposed containers.

In terms of caring for your tomato plants, regular pruning is essential. Cut off unnecessary leaves to help redirect energy towards fruit production. Don't let your plants go wild like a jungle or they'll become untidy. When it's time to harvest your tomatoes, pick them when they're ripe and bright in colour. Don't pick them prematurely or they'll taste sour. Remember, patience is important, and the wait will be worth it.

Now for the exciting part: preparing and enjoying your tomato crop. The possibilities are endless. Make some fresh tomato salads, roast them with herbs and olive oil or create delicious sauces and soups.

Growing tomatoes can be a very rewarding experience. Follow the advice above, nurture your plants like a caring gardener and watch as your tomatoes grow. Remember, with patience and care you'll soon be enjoying the delicious fruits of your labour.

31 In paragraph 2, what does writer say gardeners should do to grow tomatoes successfully?

    A keep the temperature in the location cool
    B choose the best location and atmosphere for the plants
    C grow the plants indoors before putting them outside
    D make sure that the plants receive plenty of sunlight

32 What should gardeners remember when moving young plants?

    A Moving plants can damage their young leaves.
    B Young plants should be moved slowly.
    C Plants can react badly to being touched by people's hands.
    D Plants can find the process of being moved disturbing.

33 How should gardeners prepare their garden for their tomato plants?

    A They should add organic matter to the soil.
    B They should dig the ground thoroughly before moving plants.
    C They should replace their garden soil with new soil from a garden centre.
    D They should water the ground frequently.

34 Why would gardeners choose to grow their tomatoes in a greenhouse?

    A The temperature is warmer than growing plants outside.
    B The plants are protected from the weather.
    C Plants will produce tomatoes for a longer period of time.
    D The air in a greenhouse is fresher than outside.

35 What does the writer advise gardeners who do not have large growing areas?

    A To use containers on a patio or a balcony.
    B To choose plants that produce small tomatoes.
    C Not to use hanging baskets as they are unsuitable.
    D To find a way which suits their approach to gardening

36 Why does the writer advise gardeners to cut some leaves off their plants?

    A It helps the plants to produce a better crop of tomatoes.
    B Too many leaves make the growing area look messy.
    C Plants tend to grow more leaves than they need.
    D Fewer leaves on a plant make harvesting the fruit easier.

Part 6

You are going to read an article about a popular hobby. Six sentences have been removed from the article. Choose from sentences **A–G** the one that fits each gap (**37–43**). There is one sentence you do not need to use.

The Joy of Bird Watching

As the sun gently rises over the picturesque landscapes of the United Kingdom, a familiar song fills the air, signalling the start of a new day. **37** [ ] There is a thrill that comes with being a bird-watching fan, a passion that first captured my interest as a small boy. Allow me to share with you this delightful hobby and say why I believe everyone should experience its charm.

Bird watching, or 'birding' as it is often called, is an activity that is bigger than just observation. **38** [ ] For me, the attraction lies in the sense of connection it creates between humanity and the natural world. Through binoculars, we are given a look into another universe.

What truly sets bird watching apart is the deep sense of calm it creates. **39** [ ] The simple act of walking through nature brings a much-needed rest from the chaos of daily life. With each step, worries are put aside and replaced by a sense of wonder as we encounter the avian treasures that live in these precious ecosystems.

Bird watching is said to develop a deep appreciation for the complex beauty of nature. The diversity of bird species that we find in our country is breathtaking, from the colourful feathers of the kingfisher to the majestic flight of birds of prey. **40** [ ]

As we become aware of the small differences in each species, we are shown the delicate balance of ecosystems and the importance of preserving them for future generations.

Perhaps the greatest gift bird watching gives us is the element of surprise. **41** [ ] The excitement of spotting a rare bird, one that few others have seen, is an adrenaline rush like no other. This gives us a sense of achievement and adds to the desire to explore further.

While it may seem complicated at first, bird watching is an activity that can be enjoyed by all. **42** [ ] All that is needed is an open heart and a sense of curiosity. The beauty of birding is that it can be done by anyone. Whether you live in a busy city or a rural village, there is always a world of birds waiting to be discovered right outside your door.

By becoming involved in bird watching, we open the doors to endless possibilities. It offers a new appreciation of the natural world and a deeper understanding of our place within it. We develop a strong sense of responsibility for looking after the natural world we see around us.

A In a world with the constant background noise of technology, losing yourself in the beauty of the natural world can be truly therapeutic.

B It is a journey into the heart of nature with an opportunity to witness the beauty of the avian world.

C Every bird has unique characteristics, which demonstrate the extraordinary artistry of evolution.

D Nature often presents us with unexpected encounters and rare sightings.

E Bird watching is a hobby that allows us to slow down and take the time to look at the world around us.

F It is the sound of our feathered friends, calling us to yet another wonderful bird-watching adventure.

G It requires no special skills or extensive knowledge.

Part 7

You are going to read four reviews of a recently published novel. For questions **43–52**, choose from the sections (**A–D**). The sections may be chosen more than once.

Which reviewer:

43	thinks the writer was more interested in using words than with telling the story well?
44	says they found the pace of the novel was inconsistent?
45	believes the writer makes readers think about life today?
46	says that after reading the novel they discussed the ideas in it with people they knew?
47	found the story of the novel too pessimistic?
48	says that they found the novel interesting because of some surprising things that happened?
49	liked the basic idea of the novel but found how it was written as a novel disappointing?
50	didn't care about what happened to the characters?
51	praises how the writer describes the characters complete with their faults?
52	found the characters in the novel simple to connect with?

The Parent by Fabio Astrella

Four people review a new novel

A. *The Parent* by Fabio Astrella is a captivating novel that explores the complex elements of modern society. Astrella skilfully investigates human relationships, presenting an examination of moral dilemmas that really make the reader think. The story develops after a man slaps a child at a family gathering, revealing the hidden tensions and secrets within the group. Astrella's writing is honest and places the reader in the lives of diverse and imperfect characters. The story-telling is fast-paced, filled with powerful moments and some unexpected events that certainly kept me interested throughout. The author represents the various points of view and emotions of each character brilliantly, making them easy to relate to. Moreover, Astrella tackles important social issues such as parenting, cultural differences and conflicts between different generations with depth and sensitivity. *The Parent* challenges your own beliefs and encouraged me to have conversations about morality and justice with friends and members of my family.

B. *The Parent* by Fabio Astrella left me disappointed and frustrated. While the concept of the story seemed interesting, the way in which it was turned into a novel was poor in my view. The plot revolves around a man slapping a child; I found the characters to be unlikable and their actions often seemed to make no sense. The characters lacked depth and were often defined by their flaws and shortcomings, making it difficult to empathise with them. Furthermore, the way the story was told felt too negative and filled with unnecessary content that added little to the overall plot. Astrella's writing style, although raw and realistic, lacked sympathy and at times became rather unpleasant. I also found the development of the story moved too fast at times and too slowly at others. In summary, *The Parent* failed to deliver and left me unsatisfied.

C. *The Parent* was a disappointing read for me. While the novel attempted to explore complex themes and issues, I found it to be unnecessarily dark and without hope. Additionally, the manner in which the writer told the story from multiple points of view only added to the confusion and, for me at least, made the story feel disjointed. There were several potentially interesting characters, but I found it difficult to connect with any of them. Fabio Astrella's writing style is certainly gritty, but he often spends too long on explanations. For me, those parts seem more about the writer showing off his vocabulary rather than adding to the story. There was also an over-use of sensational descriptions of the more shocking content of the story. To summarise, *The Parent* left me feeling disconnected and disengaged from the story and its characters, and failed to deliver a satisfying and meaningful reading experience.

D. In Fabio Astrella's most recent novel, *The Parent*, readers are presented with an honest and thought-provoking representation of contemporary life. The author's ability to capture the most important characteristics of human nature and behaviour is remarkable, as he explores complex themes like family dynamics, cultural disagreements and the sometimes unexpected consequences of our actions. The characters are excellently described, each with their own strengths and weaknesses; their personal journeys can only be described as captivating. The story of the novel is told from multiple perspectives, a technique that offers a well-rounded view of events and allows readers to empathise with each character. Astrella's writing creates a strong emotional response in the reader and leaves a lasting impression. *The Parent* is a captivating novel that prompts readers to reflect on societal and cultural issues, as well as encouraging discussions about morality and justice in today's world.

Cambridge B2 First Reading

Practice test 4

Part 5

You are going to read an article that summarises some of the issues involved in the planning of cities. For questions **31–36**, read the text below and decide which answer (**A, B, C or D**) fits best.

Trends in Urban Planning

As the speed of urbanisation continues to increase, planners and policy-makers are increasingly considering new and inventive approaches to create more environmentally-friendly and long-lasting urban environments. Three important trends in urban planning have emerged in recent years: the concept of '15-minute cities', the adoption of green planning strategies and the rise of porous cities. These trends are revolutionising the way we design and experience urban spaces, with the aim of improving the quality of life for the residents while minimising the impact on the environment.

The idea of 15-minute cities has gained significant interest in the urban-planning conversation. The phrase, which was coined by Professor Carlos Moreno, emphasises the creation of self-sufficient neighbourhoods that can meet most of people's daily needs within a 15-minute walk or bike ride from their homes. In a 15-minute city, residents have easy access to essential amenities such as schools, healthcare facilities, grocery stores, parks and workplaces. By reducing the need to travel long distances to work and encouraging active modes of transportation, 15-minute cities aim to improve community cohesion, reduce traffic congestion and improve air quality.

Green planning is another key trend in urban development. With growing concerns about environmental decline caused by climate change, cities are increasingly prioritising strategies that minimise their ecological footprint. Green planning incorporates sustainable design principles into urban infrastructure, including the use of renewable energy sources, efficient waste-management systems and the preservation of green spaces. By considering and actively including nature into urban areas, such as 'urban forests', 'green roofs' and 'vertical gardens', cities can lessen the 'heat island' effect, improve biodiversity and improve air and water quality for residents.

Porous cities, or cities that prioritise permeable surfaces, represent a huge change in urban planning. Traditionally, urban landscapes have been dominated by impermeable materials, such as concrete and asphalt that restrict natural water drainage and contribute to problems, like flooding, due to too much rain. Porous cities, on the other hand, embrace the concept of water-sensitive urban design, where surfaces allow rainwater to filter through and be absorbed into the ground. This approach helps to replenish groundwater supplies, reduce flood risks and maintain urban areas in the face of climate change. Porous pavements, rain gardens and green corridors are some of the strategies used to create permeable urban spaces.

While each of these trends has different characteristics, they often cross over and complement each other in urban-planning strategies. For instance, 15-minute cities promote the ability to walk around in your town, which not only reduces carbon emissions but also contributes to healthier communities. Green planning ideas can become features of 15-minute cities by including green spaces, such as community gardens and pocket parks, within the designated neighbourhoods. In a similar way, porous cities benefit from both 15-minute cities and green planning by reducing the need for car-dependent travel and providing natural systems to carry excess water away.

Implementing these trends requires a multi-disciplinary approach and team-work between everyone involved, including urban planners, architects, engineers, policymakers and the community. It is crucial to get residents to take part in the planning process and to ensure that their diverse needs and points of view are considered. Moreover, effective communication and knowledge-sharing platforms are essential when passing on best practices in urban planning.

Cities around the world that have welcomed these trends and included them in their future planning have become leaders in sustainable urban development. For example, Paris has made significant progress in transforming itself into a 15-minute city by assessing and improving public transportation, creating pedestrian-friendly spaces and increasing the availability of essential services within each neighbourhood. Copenhagen, known for its commitment to cycling infrastructure, is also recognised for its green planning projects, including its extensive network of green spaces and efforts to fight climate change. Singapore has also emerged as a leader in porous-city design, with its innovative approach to urban water management, which includes extensive green roofs and the collection of rainwater.

31 What is the purpose of the current trends in urban planning?

   A to increase the pace of urbanisation
   B to reduce environmental damage done by cities
   C to make the lives of the people who live in cities better
   D to invent new ways of planning cities

32 What is the main attraction of 15-minute cities for residents?

   A Residents can reach the facilities they need easily and quickly.
   B 15-minutes cities help improve the quality of the air people breathe.
   C Schools and hospitals are near to where people live.
   D It takes only 15 minutes for people to travel from one side of the city to the other.

33 In paragraph 3, what is meant by the phrase 'ecological footprint'?

   A the amount of energy communities consume
   B the damage humans do to their communities
   C the amount of waste material communities have to dispose of
   D the impact communities have on the natural environment

34 From an urban planning point of view, what is the problem with concrete surfaces?

   A They are too common in many modern cities.
   B They do not allow water to run away.
   C They contribute to the effect of climate change.
   D They make it more difficult to establish 15-minute cities.

35 What is the main point being made in paragraph 7?

   A Planners should communicate with city residents.
   B Planning decisions should be made in a disciplined way.
   C Residents of cities should be involved in planning.
   D Engineers, planners and architects should all work together.

36 Why are three cities referred to in the final paragraph?

   A They are examples of positive urban planning.
   B They are examples of 15-minute cities.
   C They have improved transport systems.
   D They have introduced green planning policies.

Part 6

You are going to read an article about the growth in popularity of women's football. Six sentences have been removed from the article. Choose from sentences **A–G** the one that fits each gap (**37–43**). There is one sentence you do not need to use.

The Rise and Evolution of Women's Football

Women's football has experienced a remarkable transformation in recent years, changing from an under-represented sport to a global sensation that has captured the attention of millions. Here, we explore the progress made by women's football, highlighting its growing popularity, increased support and its impact on gender equality in sports.

The roots of women's football can be traced back to the late 19th century when the sport gained popularity among women in England. **37**   It wasn't until the mid-20th century that women's football began to gain recognition, thanks to the determination of female players and supporters.

The breakthrough moment for women's football came in 1991 when the first Women's World Cup was held in China. **38**   The tournament's success paved the way for future growth and investment in women's football.

Since the 1990s, women's football has experienced massive growth, with increasing investment from sponsors and attention from fans. National leagues have been established in many countries, offering professional contracts and creating ways for ambitious women to develop careers. The formation of the UEFA Women's Champions League further raised the status of club football, providing high-level competition and raising overall standards.

The rising popularity of women's football has also led to a rapid increase in participation from young players. **39**   This has resulted in a larger pool of talent and a more competitive environment.

The visibility of female footballers has been crucial in inspiring young girls and challenging gender stereotypes. **40**   Their achievements on the field, combined with their support for gender equality, have helped the growth of the sport.

Women's football has played a significant role in promoting gender equality in sports. **41**   The increased visibility of women's football has contributed to broader conversations about equal pay, investment and opportunities for female athletes across all sports.

While women's football has taken tremendous steps forward, there are still challenges to overcome. **42**   However, the progress made so far indicates a promising future.

Women's football has come a long way, evolving from a marginalised sport to a global phenomenon that continues to grip audiences worldwide. The increased support, participation and representation in the sport have not only increased the power of female athletes but also challenged traditional beliefs in society and advanced gender equality.

A Gender pay gaps, inequalities in the amount of women's football broadcast on TV as well as limited investment in women's leagues remain areas that require attention.

B However, it faced opposition and was often criticised or banned due to negative social attitudes.

C It has provided the chance for women to showcase their athletic abilities, challenging assumptions about gender and sports.

D Organisations have been established to promote the sport among girls, encouraging them to take up football and providing opportunities for skill development.

E This will ensure that women's football eventually receives the recognition and support it deserves.

F The success of players like Mia Hamm, Marta, Megan Rapinoe and Ada Hegerberg, among others, has shattered 'glass ceilings' and provided aspiring athletes with strong female role models to look up to.

G This event marked a turning point in the sport's history, providing a platform for women's teams from around the world to demonstrate their skills on a global stage.

Part 7

You are going to read about one of the problems with recycling waste material. For questions **43–52**, choose from the sections (**A–D**). The sections may be chosen more than once.

Which paragraph:

43 ☐ suggests that makers should be responsible for the whole life of their products?

44 ☐ points out that recycling companies may lose business if the incorrect goods are mixed in with recyclable items?

45 ☐ includes lists of materials that could replace plastic packaging?

46 ☐ explains that a mixture of recyclable and unrecyclable goods may end up being buried in the ground?

47 ☐ suggests that consumers should find out for themselves the recycling policies in their area?

48 ☐ points out that different regions may have different recycling policies?

49 ☐ includes a list of materials that some consumers put in recycling bins even if they are not sure they can be recycled?

50 ☐ says consumers should no longer depend on products that can only be used once?

51 ☐ suggests that makers state clearly whether their products can be recycled?

52 ☐ suggests that new laws could be brought in to improve the situation?

The Pitfalls of Wish Cycling: A Vicious Cycle of Waste
Four people talk about recycling waste material

A. In the interests of protecting the environment, it is essential to adopt responsible waste-management practices. However, despite good intentions, some individuals contribute to 'wish cycling', which often has unwanted consequences and impedes recycling efforts. Wish cycling comes from a genuine desire to do the right thing for the environment. It occurs when individuals, unsure if an item can be recycled, place it in the recycling bin hoping that it will be properly sorted and recycled. Common examples include plastic bags, polystyrene foam and certain plastics that may or may not be accepted by recycling facilities. Unfortunately, wish cycling can have negative effects on the entire recycling process. One of the major resulting problems is contamination. When non-recyclable items are mixed with recyclables, they make sorting and processing material very difficult. Contamination lowers the quality of recycled materials and can make entire batches impossible to recycle. Consequently, recycling facilities have to send contaminated materials to waste landfill sites, negating the efforts of responsible recyclers.

B. A widespread lack of understanding of recycling instructions and rules contributes to wish cycling. Many individuals are unsure about what can and cannot be recycled, something that creates the mistaken belief that any item with a recycling symbol can be placed in the recycling bin. This knowledge gap highlights the need for improved education on recycling practices, including clear and accessible information regarding local recycling programmes that differ widely from area to area. When non-recyclable items are mistakenly placed in recycling bins, recycling facilities struggle to manage the materials that have been wrongly sorted. Consequently, recycling processes become less efficient, and the overall quality of recycled materials decreases. As a result, recycling companies face challenges in marketing their products, and this leads to decreased demand for recycled goods.

C. To fight against wish cycling and its negative consequences, it is necessary for us to develop an approach that considers many different factors. Firstly, and most importantly, individuals must inform themselves about local recycling services and guidelines. Education has a part to play here. Governments and recycling organisations have a vital role to play in this process by providing clear and accessible information, including online resources and recycling guides, to help people make informed decisions. Additionally, reducing waste at the source through conscious consumption behaviour is crucial. Shoppers should be persuaded to choose alternatives to plastic packaging that can be reused; alternatives such as cloth bags, goods sold in carboard packages, refillable water bottles and other containers. Individual consumers can significantly reduce the extent to which they rely on single-use items. This would have the effect of minimising the need for recycling altogether.

D. Efforts by manufacturers, policymakers and waste-management organisations are essential if recycling is to be effective. Manufacturers can play a vital role by developing more sustainable packaging solutions by reducing the use of non-recyclable materials and by clearly labelling products to inform consumers about recyclability. Policymakers in governments can introduce legislation to encourage manufacturers to take responsibility for the entire life-cycle of their products. Wish cycling, although well-intentioned, presents significant challenges to effective waste management and recycling. Contamination, increased costs and a shrinking market for recycled goods are among the negative results of wish cycling. By concentrating on education, persuading consumers to be aware of their behaviour consumption and encouraging all those involved to collaborate, we can break wish cycling behaviour and create a more sustainable future.

Answers

Part 5: Multiple choice | pages 74–85

Practise	*74*
Put it to the test 1	*77*
Put it to the test 2	*81*

Part 6: Gapped text | pages 86–91

Practise	*86*
Put it to the test 1	*88*
Put it to the test 2	*89*

Part 7: Multiple matching | pages 92–95

Practise	*92*
Put it to the test 1	*93*
Put it to the test 2	*94*

Practice tests | pages 96–103

Test 1	*96*
Test 2	*98*
Test 3	*100*
Test 4	*102*

Part 5: Practise I Answers (pages 14–15)

Q. What does the writer say about his preparation for the competition?

A He has to avoid eating too many snacks.
B He must follow a strict diet.
C He needs to eat rich food.
D He has to eat at specific times of the day.

Extract 1

Preparing for the World's Strongest Man competition is a demanding process, but it's also a rewarding one. First of all, I have to consume a lot of calories to fuel my training. I usually eat around 8,000-to-10,000 calories per day, relying on a diet that's high in protein-rich foods like lean meat, fish and eggs, carbohydrates and healthy fats. I also have to eat frequently throughout the day to reach my calorie goal, so I'm constantly snacking on things like nuts and berries in between multiple large meals.

✗ A In order reach his calorie goal, he is *constantly snacking*... This is a conscious, deliberate action.

✓ B *I have to consume ... 8,000-to-10,000 calories per day ... I have to eat frequently throughout the day...*

✗ C The foods he eats are protein-rich. These may not be 'rich foods' – foods that are full of oil, butter, eggs, cream, sugar, etc. ('rich' here is a distractor).

✗ D He doesn't eat at specific times. He says he has to *eat frequently throughout the day*... ('throughout the day' means at any time of the day).

Q. In these two paragraphs, the writer explains

A that he never allows himself to relax while he is training.
B that he concentrates solely on increasing his strength.
C that his training exercises are always painful.
D how he trains for the competition without damaging his body.

Watch out for **distractors** — information that may lead to choosing a wrong answer!

B2 Reading | Part 5 | Answers

> **Extract 2**

Building up almost super-human strength requires intense weightlifting and functional fitness exercises. I train for several hours a day, six days a week, and I focus on exercises that will help me perform well in the competition.

It's important to take care of your body while training, and I make sure to warm up properly before each workout, stretch regularly and take it easy on the days when I'm feeling particularly tired or sore. At the same time, it's essential to push yourself to reach your goals.

✗ **A** He allows himself to relax if he feels he is damaging his health: *take it easy on the days when I'm feeling particularly tired or sore*. The word 'never' makes this answer incorrect.

✗ **B** As well as increasing his strength by weightlifting, he does *functional fitness exercises and exercises that will help me perform well in the competition*. The word 'solely' is the reason that this answer is not correct.

✗ **C** The word 'always' makes this answer incorrect. The writer refers to *days when I'm feeling particularly tired or sore*. This means that there are some days when he does not feel tired or sore.

✓ **D** The first paragraph describes what he has to do to train physically. The second paragraph explains how he looks after his body at the same time as training effectively.

Q. What does the writer say about his personal relationships while he is training?

A He spends no time with friends while he is training.
B It's impossible for him to stay on good terms with people.
C There is a group of people who are sympathetic to his aims.
D He feels fortunate to have family support for what he is doing.

> **Extract 3**

Preparation for the competition requires a great deal of dedication and sacrifice, and I've had to give up some of my social life and devote all of my time and energy to training. It can also be difficult to maintain relationships with friends and family who don't understand the time and dedication required to compete at this level. But I'm lucky: I have a network of people who understand and support my goals.

✗	A	The writer says he has *had to give up some of my social life* – not all of it.
✗	B	It is not 'impossible'; *it's difficult to maintain relationships*. The phrase *to stay on good terms with* is more negative than *maintain relationships*.
✓	C	He says he has *a network of people who understand and support my goals*.
✗	D	The *network of people* he refers to is not restricted to family members.

Q. What does the writer say about the costs involved in entering competitions?

A The main expense involved is travelling all over the world.
B He doubts whether going in for this competition is good value for money.
C He spends a lot on money on creating his profile on social media.
D He is dependent on the financial support he gets from others.

Extract 4

It also costs a fortune. There are gym memberships, supplements and equipment, as well as the high cost of travel from Iceland to many different competition venues and expensive lodging for the competition. I mean, it's great to see the world while I'm competing, but it does come at a cost; I have given up a lot so I wouldn't miss out. But I have made up my mind to give my all to make it to the competition, and I believe it's worth it.

Of course, I couldn't do any of this without the support of my sponsors. It's vital to have a solid brand and a strong and constant social media presence. This allows you to showcase your achievements, training and personality to a wider audience and, for some competitors, attract potential sponsors.

✗	A	*The high cost of travel from Iceland to many different competition venues* is listed as one of the expenses involved but not the main one.
✗	B	Having listed the expense of competing, he says *I believe it's worth it*. The expression 'worth it' can also be a reference to other things he has had to give up to continue competing. The word 'value' is a distractor.
✗	C	He stresses the importance of *a strong and constant social media presence* but does not mention whether this is a financial expense.
✓	D	Having listed how expensive going in for competitions is, the writer says *I couldn't do any of this without the support of my sponsors*.

Part 5: Put it to the test 1 | Answers (pages 16–17)

31. How did the author get into gaming?

  A by playing a lot of games after school with his friends
  B by playing on a used gaming system he received
  C by playing online games with his parents
  D by playing online games with his brother

Paragraph 1

I remember when I first started playing computer games. It was back when I was just a kid, and <u>my parents had gotten me a second-hand video games console</u> for my birthday. I would rush home from school and spend hours on end playing games, as did a lot of children in my friend group, and I quickly became obsessed with them. My brother was the opposite and couldn't stand them. As I got older, I realised that gaming was more than just a hobby for me – it was a passion.

✗ A He played in his bedroom. The only mention of 'friends' is *as did a lot of children in my friend group*... They did the same as he did: they played alone.

✓ B 'used gaming system he received' – *my parents had gotten me a second-hand video games console*... This was a birthday gift ('used' = second hand).

✗ C His parents are mentioned but only because they gave him the system.

✗ D His brother was his opposite: *My brother... couldn't stand them* ('them' = the games).

Remember: In the first instance, choose the option (A, B, C or D) that you think is correct. Check your answer by trying to rule out the other three options.

32. What does the author say about his decision to become a professional gamer?

  A He made the choice very quickly.
  B His parents fully supported him.
  C His friends helped him to make the choice.
  D It took him a long time to decide.

Paragraph 2

That's how I ended up gaming professionally. It wasn't an easy decision to make, and I thought long and hard about it, but I knew that I had the skills to compete at a high level. I have to admit that it took a lot of effort to persuade my parents to take it seriously, but their opinion meant more to me than any opinion of my friends. My father wasn't pleased when I told him my plan was to keep on playing games in my bedroom! I started competing in local tournaments, and, as I gained more experience and success I decided to take my talents to the next level.

✗   **A**   He did not make the choice quickly — he *thought long and hard about it.*

✗   **B**   His parents didn't support him fully — *it took a lot of me persuading my parents to take it seriously / My father wasn't pleased.*

✗   **C**   He refers to friends but only to say that their opinion was less important than his parents' opinion.

✓   **D**   'the decision to become a professional gamer' — *It wasn't an easy decision to make, and I thought long and hard about it.*

---

33. What does the author do to make money from gaming?

   A   He has yet to make money.

   B   He is sponsored by a major brand.

   C   He relies on his fans to pay him.

   D   He has several sources of income.

Paragraph 3

As a professional gamer, I earn money through various ways such as from winning tournament prizes, advertising money from streaming my games on websites such as Twitch or YouTube (plus online videos talking about the games) and even donations from fans. My dream would be for a big company to sponsor me, but that's a long way off. This industry is growing rapidly, and the potential for earning money as a professional gamer is increasing. However, it requires commitment, talent and hard work to succeed in this competitive field. And I'm 100% committed – I couldn't imagine doing anything else.

✗	A	'He has yet to make money' means he does not earn already. The text contradicts this: *As a professional gamer, I **earn** money...*
✗	B	Being sponsored is something he hopes for in the future: *My dream would be for a big company to sponsor me, but that's a long way off.*
✗	C	He does not rely on his fans to pay: *even donations from fans* are one of his sources of income. The word '*even*' suggests that it is not a regular or reliable source of come. These are donations, rather than payments.
✓	D	'several sources of income' – *winning tournament prizes, advertising money from streaming my games on websites...*

---

34. In line 20, what does 'my days are a balancing act' mean?

- A   The author feels the pressure to perform for his fans.
- **B   The author has to manage many things simultaneously.**
- C   The author has days where he has to do competitions and promotion.
- D   The author needs to manage gaming and another job.

Paragraph 4

Nowadays, <u>my days are a balancing act between practising, streaming my games to my audience, and responding to comments from my followers and taking breaks</u> to avoid getting too tired. When I get into my game setup in the morning, I fill out my schedule for the day – I might spend a few hours practising for the next competition, reviewing past games or taking part in online tournaments.

✗	A	No reference to his feeling pressure from fans (*followers*), although he does spend *some time responding to comments from my followers.*
✓	B	He does a lot of things at the same time ('simultaneously'): *my days are a balancing act between practising, streaming my games ... responding to comments from my followers ... taking breaks.*
✗	C	The writer does not say he **has** to do competitions. This would suggest pressure. He says: *my schedule for the day – I might spend a few hours practising for the next competition.* The word '*might*' suggests it's a possible part of his schedule.
✗	D	There is no suggestion that the writer does another job.

35. In the fifth paragraph, the author talks about gaming and says that he

   A   doesn't enjoy it as much as he used to.
   B   thinks he will probably need to quit gaming soon.
   | C   usually enjoys it but sometimes it's not so much fun. |
   D   knows he has quite a heavy addiction to it.

Paragraph 5

Despite how much I love gaming, there are times when I do get bored of it. Some people get addicted to video games, and it can be hard for them to step away from the screen. But when I feel that way, I know it's time to quit for a while and focus on something else. The cycling helps with this, but I also like to read or do some drawing.

✗   A   There is no indication in the blog that the author enjoys it less than he did. He says: *Despite how much I love gaming...*

✗   B   The author admits that, if he thinks he may be getting addicted: *I know it's time to quit for a while and focus on something else.*

✓   C   *Despite how much I love gaming... I do get bored of it.*

✗   D   The author makes the point that **he** doesn't get addicted: *Some people get addicted to video games.*

---

36. Which games does the author say are his favourites?

   | A   The games that made him fall in love with gaming. |
   B   The competitive multi-player games.
   C   The games that are the most popular at the time.
   D   The games that can make him the most money.

Paragraph 6

The choice of which game to play can depend on various factors such as personal preference, skill level and the current popularity of a game. Some games can make professionals more money than others – financially, the big multi-player battle games are the ones to get into. As for my personal favourite, it's hard to choose just one. There are so many incredible games out there, each with their unique strengths and weaknesses. However, I have a particular love for League of Monsters and all the games that made me try competitive gaming.

B2 Reading | Part 5 | Answers

✓ **A** ...*I have a particular love for League of Monsters and all the games that made me try competitive gaming* ('particular love' = favourites)

✗ **B** He says *financially, the big, multi-player battle games are the ones to get into*... but not that these games are his favourites.

✗ **C** He refers to *the current popularity of a game* (games that are the most popular at the time), but not that these are his favourites.

✗ **D** There is no reference to earning money in this part of the blog.

Part 5: Put it to the test 2 | Answers (pages 18–19)

31. What led to the author becoming a midwife?

   A She loved being around babies.
   B She wanted to help other people.
   C She worked as a doctor before specialising.
   D She felt inspired by what she experienced at nursing school.

Paragraph 2

Alhough I've always loved babies, I decided to go into this profession because <u>I have always had a passion for helping others</u>. After finishing high school, I considered going to medical college to become a doctor, but in the end I did a nursing degree. I then went on to specialise in midwifery, which I knew immediately <u>was the right decision</u>. It was the perfect fit for me because I wanted to work in a field where I could <u>make a difference in people's lives</u>, and being a midwife allows me to do just that.

✗ **A** The author says *I've always loved babies*... but her main motivation is helping people, especially new parents.

✓ **B** ...*have always had a passion for helping others*.

✗ **C** She didn't work as a doctor... *I considered going to medical college to become a doctor*...

✗ **D** She does not mention *nursing school* or *inspiration*, but did *a nursing degree*.

Note: 'doctor' is a distractor. She didn't go to medical college.

32. In the third paragraph, the author explains that the best part of her job is

    A seeing a parent's reaction to their new baby.

    B the salary she is paid

    C the flexibility to work when she wants.

    D being there when the baby arrives.

Paragraph 3

It's not the best-paid job and my schedule depends on other people, <u>but</u> I wouldn't change it. <u>The most amazing part of my job is being present for the birth of a baby</u>.

✗   A There is no mention of parents' reaction to births.

✗   B *It's not the most well-paid job...* **but** *I wouldn't change it*

✗   C There is no flexibility. She says: *my schedule depends on other people...*

✓   D *The most amazing part of my job is being present for the birth of a baby.*

Note: The word 'but' shows that being well-paid is not important.

---

33. What does the author say about her relationships with her patients?

    A She enjoys helping and informing new mothers.

    B She usually only sees patients for their first child.

    C She often sees new parents lose confidence.

    D She is very involved in the weeks after the baby arrives.

Paragraph 5

Being a midwife, I love the relationships I build with my patients. It's not unusual for me to see the same women for several pregnancies, and it's always a joy to see how their families grow and change over time. Although I tend to be a bit hands-off after the birth, <u>I still love being able to provide education and support to new mothers</u>, and to see the <u>confidence</u> they gain as they become more comfortable in their roles as parents.

B2 Reading | Part 5 | Answers

✓   **A**   *...love being able to provide education and support to new mothers...*

✗   **B**   She sometimes sees the same mother several times: *...not unusual for me to see the same women for several pregnancies...*

✗   **C**   This answer is the opposite of what she says: *...see the confidence they gain.* To 'gain' **confidence** is the opposite of to 'lose' confidence.

✗   **D**   She is not very involved after the baby arrives: *Although I tend to be a bit hands-off after the birth...* ('hands-off' means the opposite of 'involved').

> **Note:** 'confidence' is a distractor.

---

34. By attending a variety of births, the author has been

     A   surprised that births often go more smoothly in a hospital setting.

     B   interested to find out that births usually require hospital involvement.

     C   surprised that births can be completely different for each person.

     D   interested to learn that births are different if the mother is a very active person.

Paragraph 6

I've had the pleasure of attending a variety of births, from natural home births to hospital births with medical assistance. It's always a new experience <u>to see the different ways women choose to give birth</u>, and I've learned a lot from each experience. Last week alone I had one patient who was a professional athlete and continued running up until the day she gave birth, and another patient who came in to have one baby and left with twins!

✗   **A**   The author mentions hospital settings but does not suggest that births go more smoothly in hospital – *...variety of births, from natural home births to hospital births...*

✗   **B**   The author mentions that hospital settings *include medical assistance...* but not that hospital births **require** this.

✓   **C**   *It's always a new experience to see the different ways women choose to give birth.* This suggests **surprise**.

✗   **D**   She refers to a mother who is very active (a professional athlete) but not that this makes births different.

JoEnglish Let's Go Cambridge! B2 First Reading and Listening

35. In line 25, 'think on your feet' means

   A to know how to deal with delivery issues safely.
   B to carefully follow the birth plan.
   C to be able to move around while working.
   D to react as necessary at the time.

Paragraph 7

However, in this line of work it's important to be able to think on your feet because things can change quickly during labour and delivery. It's crucial to be able to adapt to new situations as they come up. In the past, I've had to cancel birth plans and make quick decisions based on the safety of both mother and baby.

✗   A   Thinking about safety is important, but this is not 'think on your feet' means.

✗   B   The author mentions *cancelling birth plans...* but this is not what 'think on your feet' means.

✗   C   'Thinking on your feet' does not involve walking or any physical movement.

✓   D   ...*crucial to be able to adapt to new situations...*

36. In the final paragraph, what does the author say about her career?

   A She will be passionate about it for the remainder of her working life.
   B She thinks the hardest thing is hiding her emotions from patients.
   C She finds it difficult to give everything to her job, all of the time.
   D She feels that everyone would enjoy the job if they knew what it involved.

Paragraph 9

Even in those difficult moments, I know that I'm doing everything I can to give 100% to my patients. I realise that being a midwife is not for everyone, but for those who have a passion for it there's nothing else like it in the world. I feel incredibly lucky to be able to do what I do, and I know I will continue to find enjoyment in this career for as long as I do it. Despite how I feel, the job definitely has its challenges, like the emotions it produces in you and balancing work and personal life...

B2 Reading | Part 5 | Answers

✓   **A**   *...I know I will continue to find enjoyment in this career for as long as I do it.*

✗   **B**   She refers to her emotions but not that she hides them from patients.

✗   **C**   She says she gives everything: *I know that I'm doing everything I can to give 100% to my patients – Even in those difficult moments* – in other words: all of the time.

✗   **D**   She knows not everyone would enjoy her job: *I realise that being a midwife is not for everyone...*

JoEnglish Let's Go Cambridge! B2 First Reading and Listening

Part 6: Practise | Answers   (pages 22–23)

Extract 1

The TV quiz programme 'Who Wants to Be a Millionaire?' is essentially a knowledge-based game show that tests the intelligence, quick thinking and bravery of its contestants. **This show consists of a series of multiple-choice questions of increasing difficulty, with a choice of four possible answers for each question.** Contestants must choose the correct option to continue in the game and eventually try to win the top prize.

| 1 | D |

'choice' = option

One of the show's most famous features is the system of lifelines*, which provide contestants with assistance when they encounter challenging questions. **The most well-known of these* is 'Phone-a-Friend', which lets contestants call a chosen individual for help.** The 'Ask the Audience' lifeline allows contestants to rely on the combined knowledge of the studio audience, and '50:50' removes two incorrect answers, leaving the contestant with a 50% chance of choosing the correct option. These lifelines add an element of strategy to the game, as contestants must decide when and how to use them effectively.

| 2 | C |

* *The most well-known of these... 'these' = these lifelines*

The success of 'Who Wants to Be a Millionaire?' is due not only to its engaging gameplay but also in the charm of its hosts. Throughout the show's history, there have been many different hosts, each bringing their own unique style and personality. From the popular original host, Chris Tarrant, who was presenter of the UK version for 15 years, to the current UK host Jeremy Clarkson, each host has left their mark on the show*. **Their humour** and ability to build excitement keep viewers on the edge of their seats, improving the overall experience of both TV and studio audiences.**

| 3 | A |

* *...mark on the show... = the missing sentence describes marks presenters leave.*
** *Their humour... = the humour of the presenters referred to in the text.*

Sentence B does not fit any of the gaps. The subject matter could relate to missing sentence D, which refers to the level of difficulty of the questions. The word *these* does not refer back to anything earlier.

B2 Reading | Part 6 | Answers

Extract 2

In addition to its television success, the show has expanded into other forms of media. **It has inspired board games and computer games, allowing fans to experience the excitement of the competition themselves.** These adaptations* provide an interactive experience, in which players can test their knowledge and decision-making skills just like the show's contestants. The popularity of these games demonstrates the enduring appeal of 'Who Wants to Be a Millionaire?' beyond the television screen. Furthermore, the franchise's influence has even extended to the big screen with the world-famous film 'Slumdog Millionaire'.

| 1 | C |

* These adaptations = ...board games and computer games...

Furthermore, the franchise's influence has even extended to the big screen with the world-famous film 'Slumdog Millionaire'. Directed by Danny Boyle, the movie tells the story of Jamal Malik, a young boy who appears on the Indian version of 'Who Wants to Be a Millionaire'. **The film explores the life experiences that help the youngster answer the quiz questions** correctly.

| 2 | D |

The use of the definite article 'the' in '...**the** youngster...' refers back to the first mention of '...**a** young boy...' in the text.

According to well-known psychologist Dr. Sarah Johnson, 'Who Wants to Be a Millionaire?' connects with our human brains in a way that makes it fascinating for both contestants and viewers. **She explains that the way the show works brings together elements of knowledge-testing, decision-making under pressure and the appeal of a life-changing reward.** This combination* creates a powerful mixture of excitement and tension that causes the release of chemicals in the brain. The expectation of a potential million-pound prize stimulates...

| 3 | A |

* This combination... = the missing sentence brings together elements of knowledge-testing, decision-making under pressure and the appeal of a life-changing reward.

Sentence B does not fit any of the gaps. The subject of the sentence 'She' is someone who wins the top prize, but the only person in the text who wins the top prize is the boy in the film 'Slumdog Millionaire'. The only 'she' referred to in the text is Dr Sarah Johnson, a psychologist, not a contestant in a show.

JoEnglish Let's Go Cambridge! B2 First Reading and Listening

Part 6: Put it to the test 1 | Answers   (pages 24–25)

The Covid-19 pandemic has had a huge impact on education worldwide, particularly in developing countries. While some of these countries were able to adapt quickly to online learning and remote teaching, others were not so lucky, leaving many students struggling to keep up with their studies. In this report, we will examine the impact of the pandemic on education in the developing world, with a focus on six specific countries.

37 | C

Further reading of the text shows that the six specific countries are those that were 'not so lucky'.

At the beginning of the pandemic, many developing countries were forced to close schools and pause face-to-face learning. This was a huge problem for a significant number of students who were already struggling to get by on limited resources. Online education was not an option for many of these students due to a lack of internet access, computers, and other necessary equipment.

38 | G

...close schools... = This was a huge problem ('This' refers back to school closures).

Similarly, in Pakistan, where many students rely on public schools, the pandemic put children's education at risk. According to a recent survey conducted by the National Education Association, 30% of Pakistani students did not attend online classes due to a lack of resources, while others struggled to keep up with the pace of online learning.

39 | A

Nigeria is the subject of the previous paragraph. The missing sentence starts with 'Similarly'. The writer is comparing Pakistan with Nigeria. The text and the missing sentence both mention Pakistan.

However, despite these challenges, many developing countries have been working to make up for lost time and to find ways to help students catch up with their studies. In Bangladesh, for example, the government has provided free online education to students during the pandemic and has distributed radios and televisions to those who do not have internet access.

40 | E

This paragraph compares Bangladesh favourably with Afghanistan. Bangladesh has managed to help children by providing resources not available in Afghanistan. The word 'However' introduces an idea that contrasts with what has gone before.

In Myanmar, where the pandemic has put the education of millions of children at risk, the government has been working to provide all students with access to online education. **It has been working with international organisations to provide devices and internet access to students who lack these resources.**

The pronoun 'It' refers back to 'government' in the previous sentence.

Despite these efforts, there is still much work to be done to ensure that students in developing countries are not left behind due to the pandemic. **One major help would be for governments and organisations to take account of the unique challenges facing students in these countries and provide the necessary support to help them catch up with their studies.** They must also continue to explore alternative approaches to education and provide resources to help students get over the impact of the pandemic on their mental health and well-being.

If students are 'left behind', they need to 'catch up'.

Sentence D does not fit any of the gaps. Governments and other organisations are mentioned in the text but not NGOs (Non-governmental organisations). The word 'The' in sentence D would be referring back to a previous mention.

Part 6: Put it to the test 2 | Answers   (pages 26–27)

The world of buying and selling sports shoes has become a crazy and highly profitable industry. **In recent years, it has brought in a new word to describe people involved in the industry.** 'Sneakerheads', as they are often called, are people who collect and trade rare or limited-edition sneakers, and who are willing to pay a lot of money for the most unique pairs. Here, we will explore the ins and outs of the sneaker market and highlight a successful seller who has made a name for himself in this highly competitive industry.

The pronoun 'it' in the missing sentence refers back to 'industry' in the text.
'word' in the missing sentence is named as 'Sneakerheads' in the text.

To start with, the sneaker market has become a global phenomenon, with buyers and sellers all over the world. **Many sneakerheads set up their own online stores or social media accounts to show their collections and attract potential buyers.** Some even figure out ways to create unofficial versions of highly rare sneakers in order to buy up stock at lower prices and sell on at a significant profit.

38	F

'buyers and sellers' in the text are referred to as 'sneakerheads' in the missing sentence.
'Some' refers to a number of the 'Many sneakerheads' mentioned in the missing sentence.

Sneakerheads are typically looking for rare or limited-edition sneakers, especially those with a unique design, history or connection to a well-known brand or artist. **They may also be interested in old or classic sneakers that have become highly popular and searched for over time.** Some examples of sneakers that sneakerheads might look out for include the Nike Air Jordan 1, Adidas Yeezy Boost and the Converse Chuck Taylor All-Star.

39	A

'They' in the missing sentence refers to 'Sneakerheads' in the first part of the text.
'also' in 'also be interested' in the missing sentence is in addition to 'rare or limited-edition sneakers' in the text.

In 2023, a pair of game-worn Nike Air Jordan sneakers sold for a record $2.2 million, making it the most expensive sneaker ever sold. **It is worth noting, however*, that most sneakerheads so not spend such high amounts on their collections, and there are many sneakers available at lower prices**** for those who are interested in the hobby.

40	E

'such high amounts' in the missing sentence refers to '$2.2 million' in the text.
* 'however' in the missing sentence points out contrasting information.
** 'at lower prices' means lower than the high prices mentioned previously.

One example of a successful sneaker trader is Benjamin Kickz, who is known as the 'Sneaker Don'. He started his business at the young age of 13 by buying and selling shoes online. He quickly made connections in the industry and started shopping around for rare and exclusive sneakers He used to jump into queues, paying huge amounts of money to get his hands on limited-edition pairs. **As his reputation grew, he started to make a name for himself among the celebrity crowd, with clients such as Drake, DJ Khaled and Chris Brown.** Benjamin Kickz later expanded into clothing and jewellery as well.

41	C

B2 Reading | Part 6 | Answers

'Benjamin Kickz' is described as 'a successful sneaker trader' in the text, who manages to 'make a name for himself' in the missing sentence.

'his reputation' in the missing sentence refers to 'Benjamin Kickz' earlier and later in the text, and all the uses of the pronoun 'he'.

The sneaker industry is highly competitive and can be challenging, unless you have a reputation like Benjamin. **Successful sellers like him² know that they must bear in mind the latest trends and keep an eye on the market to stay ahead.** A well-timed phone call or message to their network of contacts can keep them informed and maintain their position as a top seller.

| 42 | G |

Successful sellers must keep an eye on the market to maintain their position as a top seller because the sneaker market is highly competitive.

Successful sellers like him in the missing sentence refers to Benjamin (Kickz) in the text.

Sentence B does not fit any of the gaps. The initial word it in Sentence B does not relate to anything in any of the sentences preceding any of the gaps. The paragraph that includes Gap 38 mentions social media and the paragraph that contains Gap 41 mentions a successful sneakerhead, but these are distractors as there are no specific language links.

Part 7: Practise 1 | Answers (pages 30–31)

1. Which person worked with teenagers?

   Text B: ...*camp was designed for curious minds* **between the ages of 12 and 15**... — 1 B

2. Which person worked with children with scientific interests?

   Text B: ...*who were enthusiastic about* **science, technology, engineering**... — 2 B

3. Which person mentions a weekly competition?

   Text A: ...*the sports* **tournament** *held at the end of* **each week**. — 3 A
   ('tournament' = competition)

4. Which person tried to develop children's ability to solve problems?

   Text B: ...*encouraged critical thinking and* **problem-solving skills**... — 4 B

5. Which person mentions that children's relatives saw what they had done?

   Text B: ...*demonstrated their individual projects to other children and* **their parents**. — 5 B

6. Which person encouraged children to work together in groups?

   Text A: ...*working* **as a team**. — 6 A

Part 7: Practise 2 | Answers (pages 32–33)

1. Which person describes how the children felt proud of what they achieved?

   Text B: *You could see the sense of* **achievement and pride that showed**... — 1 B

2. Which person mentions that children made something unusual for people to wear?

   Text B: ...*creating* **unique jewellery**... — 1 B

3. Which person describes a camp situated in a wooded area?

   Text A: ...*located in the middle of a picturesque* **forest, surrounded by tall trees**... — 3 A

4. Which person describes activities that encouraged children to work together?

   Text B: ...*projects that required* **cooperation and the children to work in teams**. — 4 B

5. Which person describes how the children became more confident due to their experience?

   Text B: ...*develop their communication skills and increase their confidence*.

   | 5 | B |

6. Which person mentions that their group camped at night?

   Text A: ...*overnight camping trip. We set up tents*...

   | 6 | A |

Part 7: Put it to the test 1 | Answers (pages 34–35)

43. Which person mentions that they work somewhere that sells used items at a discount?

    Text B: ...*charity shop worker ... variety of unwanted items that come into the shop that can now be sold for much less*...

    | 43 | B |

44. Which person believes that helping those who have been affected by social or political violence is very satisfying?

    Text C: *Syria*...*conflict in the country ... displaced by the conflict ... such difficult circumstances*.

    | 44 | C |

45. Which person describes how volunteering allows them to meet people from different backgrounds?

    Text A: *people from all walks of life* = people with different types of jobs and from different levels of society.

    | 45 | A |

46. Which person finds that volunteering is a great way to spend time now that they've finished work?

    Text B: *It's a great way to keep busy now that I'm retired.*
    (to be 'retired' = to have finished working, usually on reaching a certain age)

    | 46 | B |

47. Which person states that their listening skills are crucial for their volunteering work?

    Text D: *The ability to listen patiently is key ... By being sympathetic and listening, we can help make a difference in someone's life*...
    ('key' and 'crucial' = very important)

    | 47 | D |

48. Which person says that they're always curious about the range of things that end up at their charity shop?

    Text B: *It's always interesting to see the variety of items that come into the shop*...

    | 48 | B |

49. Which person suggests that the speed of modern life can make people feel alone?

   Text D: ...the world being so fast-moving and stressful, it's easy for people to feel lonely...

   | 49 | D |

50. Which person thinks that they have learned to appreciate everything they have because of their volunteer work?

   Text C: ...(the work) reminds me to be grateful for the simple things I have in my life.
   (In this context, 'to be grateful for' = to appreciate)

   | 50 | C |

51. Which person explains that they will return to their studies after their volunteer work?

   Text C: Taking a year out from university ... and take part in volunteer work.
   (It is sometimes called a gap year = when students leave the place of study for a time, then go back after the 'gap'.)

   | 51 | C |

52. Which person says that it's important not to judge those that need help?

   Text A: It's essential to treat everyone with kindness and respect whatever their circumstances.

   | 52 | A |

Part 7: Put it to the test 2 | Answers   (pages 36–37)

43. Which person explains that cats have bad attitudes?

   Text C: For me, cats are so arrogant ... a cat would eat you if they could. ...judging your every move.

   | 43 | C |

44. Which person thinks that it's nice when a cat doesn't demand affection?

   Text A: I respect cats for their independence. ...when they're not in the mood for socialising, but that's just part of their charm.

   | 44 | A |

45. Which person mentions that they have several pets?

   Text B: I have a pack of dogs...

   | 45 | B |

46. Which person believes that despite the attention of strangers, their pets' appearance isn't important?

   Text B: It's enjoyable for me to see how nice they look and how much attention they get from the public. But, at the end of the day, it's not about how my dogs look...

   | 46 | B |

Watch out for distractors — information that may lead to choosing a wrong answer!

B2 Reading | Part 7 | Answers

47. Which person suggests that looking after a dog would take up more time than a cat?

   Text C: *Secondly, let's talk about **energy levels**. **Dogs will play until they get tired**, and then **they'll still want to go for a walk**.*

   | 47 | C |

48. Which person states that cats demand much less attention than dogs?

   Text A: *...**dogs can be so needy (whereas cats) don't need constant attention or approval**...*

   | 48 | A |

49. Which person sounds as though they're trying to justify the idea of getting a pet?

   Text D: *I've been **unsure about having a pet, but if I were to get one**, I think I would go for a cat. I don't have any pets at the moment... **the more I think about it**...*

   | 49 | D |

50. Which person finds that training a pet is essential to avoid trouble?

   Text A: *To me, **dogs can do more harm than good**, especially **if they're not taught properly**.*

   | 50 | A |

51. Which person believes that cats are less energetic than dogs?

   Text C: *...let's talk about **energy levels**. Good luck trying to get a cat to fetch something or go for a run. **Dogs will play until they get tired** ... They'll (cats) **sit on the arm of the sofa**...*

   | 51 | C |

52. Which person explains that their pets are a good way of staying healthy?

   Text B: *...they're (dogs) the perfect excuse for a **good walk**. My **dogs keep me fit and active**...*

   | 52 | B |

95

JoEnglish Let's Go Cambridge! B2 First Reading and Listening

Practise test 1 | Answers (pages 41–48)

Part 5		Key words from the questions	Clues from the text
31	C	They have a variety of life experiences	from many different backgrounds
32	A	She had heard other travellers' accounts of making the journey	The stories of self-discovery / had fascinated her for years
33	D	Making meaningful contact with so many different people.	Maria had serious conversations with these diverse individuals
34	B	Everything she has to think about during her home life.	disconnect from the noise of daily life and focus on my inner thoughts
35	C	make more contact with people in the areas the route went through.	more time interacting with the locals and immersing myself in the culture of the regions I passed through.
36	B	the walk had improved her physical condition	I had not considered how much my general fitness would benefit

Part 6		Key words from the questions	Clues from the text
37	B	It has been a battleground	chess has been more than simply a game
38	C	this new interest / new technology and the rise of media platforms.	This development
39	E	These platforms have created a global	Platforms like chess.com / players and fans from around the world
40	G	powerful chess engines like Stockfish	revolutionising the way players study and prepare for games / These AI-powered tools
41	A	chess has found its way onto the small screen	the influence of television programmes / The Netflix mini-series
42	F	This interactive feature	now regularly livestream their matches, providing useful commentary and communicating with viewers / The popularity of chess streamers

B2 Reading | Practice test | Answers

Part 7		Key words from the questions	Clues from the text
43	D	have to play at times they would rather spend with friends and family	working on weekends and holidays, giving up personal time with my loved ones
44	A	finds it difficult to make enough money	trying to earn a living from my art has been incredibly challenging
45	C	enjoys playing with other musicians, but finds it limiting	I really want to explore my own musical ideas / it's a wonderful experience
46	B	receives some of their income from audience members	the tips from enthusiastic tourists can be generous
47	D	on celebratory occasions	wedding singer / be a part of people's special day
48	A	feels discouraged by the challenges	It's depressing / the constant uncertainty … I'm always experiencing self-doubt
49	B	pattern of work allows them time to get better at playing music	regular schedule that allows me to focus on my craft and continue improving my skills
50	A	difficult to find enough opportunities to play	There are few opportunities for gigs
51	C	no choice about what and how they play	means sticking to strict musical interpretations and following a conductor's lead
52	D	a range of very different venues	my work exciting. From small garden ceremonies to receptions in massive houses or hotels,

JoEnglish Let's Go Cambridge! B2 First Reading and Listening

Practise test 2 | Answers (pages 49–56)

Part 5		Key words from the questions	Clues from the text
31	C	affects the length of time when pollen levels are high	changing climate, which leads to longer pollen seasons
32	A	bodies respond more strongly than they should	the body's natural defence to disease, over-reacts to harmless things
33	B	their eyes react more than normal to light	can become super sensitive to light.
34	D	make their eyes and nose less painful	nasal sprays or eye drops to reduce inflammation
35	B	condition is not improved by medicines that can be bought easily	doesn't get better with over-the-counter treatments, it's a good idea to see a doctor
36	A	Some forecasts broadcast information about pollen levels	pollen levels each day / This information is sometimes included in weather forecasts

Part 6		Key words from the questions	Clues from the text
37	D	to challenge himself by running his first marathon	got him started in Extreme Marathon running / The thrill of completing that race started a desire within me
38	G	more than just physical challenges; they're a journey of self-discovery	drives him to participate in those incredibly challenging races / I believe that by pushing myself to the edge
39	A	one of the most memorable races he had participated in was the 'Desert Storm Ultra'	an example of an extreme marathon that left a lasting impression on him / This was held in the deserts of Namibia
40	F	complete determination to overcome these dangers fuelled my spirit	dehydration became a real threat / Crossing the finish line was an experience I'll remember forever.
41	B	how he stayed motivated during the long and demanding hours	mental strength required for such races must be huge / Mental strength is undoubtedly crucial.

| 42 | E | I research the course, understand the potential dangers involved | Safety is the most important thing / I also equip myself with the correct gear |

Part 7		Key words from the questions	Clues from the text
43	B	learn a lot about digital technology in a short time	their learning curve for digital tools has been steeper
44	C	time when the economy was unpredictable	We grew up during a time of economic instability
45	A	educated in a rather old-fashioned way	We relied on traditional teaching methods
46	D	understand how shoppers think and act	understanding of online platforms and consumer behaviour
47	B	appreciates having grown up in a technologically advanced world	am grateful for the technological developments that have shaped our lives
48	A	capable of doing many things simultaneously	displaying remarkable multi-tasking abilities
49	B	able to make links between digital technology and older ways of working	bridge the gap between traditional methods and digital innovation
50	C	understands the need to plan for the future?	keen understanding of risk management, long-term planning
51	D	their generation is both imaginative and technically capable makes them different	Our ability to use creativity with technology equally well sets us apart
52	D	Generation X has had to get used to the idea that business can be done digitally	Generation X has had to adapt to the rise of digital marketing

Practise test 3 | Answers   (pages 57–64)

Part 5		Key words from the questions	Clues from the text
31	B	the best location and atmosphere	a suitable environment
32	D	Plants find the process of being moved disturbing	plants feel shock when they are transplanted
33	A	add organic matter to the soil	enriching it with compost – the decaying remains of other plants, or manure
34	C	produce tomatoes for a longer period of time	extension of the tomato-growing season
35	B	choose plants that produce small tomatoes	Select plants that will not grow large fruits
36	A	helps the plants to produce a better crop of tomatoes	to help redirect energy towards fruit production

Part 6		Key words from the questions	Clues from the text
37	F	sound of our feathered friends	a familiar song fills the air,
38	B	heart of nature; an opportunity to witness the beauty of the avian world	is an activity that is bigger than just observation / For me, the attraction lies in the sense of connection it creates between humanity and the natural world.
39	A	In a world with the constant background noise of technology	bird watching apart is the deep sense of calm it creates / The simple act of walking through nature
40	C	Every bird has unique characteristics	colourful feathers of the kingfisher to the majestic flight of birds of prey
41	D	unexpected encounters	watching gives us is the element of surprise / The excitement of spotting

| 42 | G | It requires no special skills or extensive knowledge | an activity that can be enjoyed by all / All that is needed is an open heart and a sense of curiosity |

Part 7		Key words from the questions	Clues from the text
43	C	more interested in using words than with telling the story well	showing off his vocabulary rather than adding to the story
44	B	found the pace of the novel was inconsistent	development of the story moved too fast at times and too slowly at others
45	D	writer makes readers think about life today	thought-provoking representation of contemporary
46	A	they discussed the ideas in it with people they knew	to have conversations about morality and justice with friends and members of my family
47	C	the story of the novel too pessimistic	be unnecessarily dark and without hope
48	A	found the novel interesting because of some surprising things that happened	some unexpected events that certainly kept me interested
49	B	liked the basic idea of the novel but found how it was written as a novel disappointing?	the concept of the story seemed interesting, the way in which it was turned into a novel was poor
50	B	didn't care about what happened to the characters	uninterested in the fate of the characters
51	D	praises how the writer describes the characters complete with their faults	characters are excellently described, each with their own strengths and weaknesses
52	A	characters in the novel simple to connect with	making them easy to relate to

JoEnglish Let's Go Cambridge! B2 First Reading and Listening

Practise test 4 | Answers   (pages 65–72)

Part 5		Key words from the questions	Clues from the text
31	C	make the lives of the people who live in cities better	improving the quality of life for the residents
32	A	reach the facilities they need easily and quickly	neighbourhoods that can meet most of people's daily needs within a 15-minute walk or bike ride from their homes
33	D	impact communities have on the natural environment	Green planning incorporates sustainable design principles / efficient waste-management / preservation of green spaces.
34	B	do not allow water to run away	impermeable materials, such as concrete and asphalt 34 which restrict natural water drainage
35	C	residents of cities should be involved in planning	crucial to get residents to take part in the planning process
36	A	examples of positive urban planning	Paris has made significant progress in transforming itself into a 15-minute city / Copenhagen, known for its commitment to cycling infrastructure / Singapore has also emerged as a leader in porous-city design

Part 6		Key words from the questions	Clues from the text
37	B	However, it faced opposition	the sport gained popularity among women in England. / It wasn't until the mid-20th century
38	G	This event marked a turning point	the first Women's World Cup was held in China / The tournament's success
39	D	Organisations have been established to promote the sport among girls	increase in participation from young players / This has resulted in a larger pool
40	F	The success of players like Mia Hamm and Ada Hegerberg has broken through 'glass ceilings' / strong female role models.	The visibility of female footballers has been crucial / Their achievements on the field

41	C	It has provided... / ... challenging assumptions about gender and sports	Women's football has played a significant role in promoting gender equality in sports / The increased visibility ... has contributed to broader conversations about equal pay
42	A	Gender pay gaps, inequalities / areas that require attention	there are still challenges to overcome / However, the progress made so far

Part 7		Key words from the questions	Clues from the text
43	D	responsible for the whole life	take responsibility for the entire life-cycle of their products
44	B	recycling companies may lose business	leads to decreased demand for recycled goods
45	C	lists of materials that could replace plastic packaging	alternatives such as cloth bags, goods sold in carboard packages and refillable water bottles
46	A	mixture of recyclable and unrecyclable goods may end up being buried in the ground?	recycling facilities have to send contaminated materials to waste landfill sites
47	C	consumers should find out for themselves the recycling policies	inform themselves about local recycling services and guidelines
48	B	different regions may have different recycling policies	local recycling programmes that differ widely from area to area
49	A	list of materials that some consumers put in recycling bins	plastic bags, polystyrene foam and certain plastics that may or may not be accepted by recycling
50	C	no longer depend on products that can only be used once	reduce the extent to which they rely on single-use items
51	D	state clearly whether their products can be recycled	Manufacturers can play a vital role ... by clearly labelling products to inform consumers about recyclability
52	D	new laws could be brought in to improve the situation	governments can introduce legislation

Tutti gli strumenti necessari per un apprendimento efficace

Non si può imparare una lingua solo studiando la grammatica o solo la pronuncia, ci vuole sinergia tra vari elementi per creare un approccio completo. Per questo motivo abbiamo creato JoEnglish.com, il primo ed unico AMBIENTE COMPLETO a 360° gradi che ti offre gli strumenti per imparare l'inglese online.

+250 lezioni ed attività
Interattive in costante aggiornamento

Live Lessons
2 volte alla settimana lezioni live direttamente con Joe e la sua famiglia

JoEnglish Podcast
100+ episodi del JoEnglish Podcast con esercizi e testo

Sessioni di conversazione
In gruppi ristretti per praticare la lingua in casi reali

Tantissimi contenuti extra
Esercizi in PDF stampabili, +10 lezioni del corso di pronuncia e il Vocabolario interattivo con +18 argomenti.

Esami Cambridge B2
Corsi di preparazione per esami Cambridge livello B2

In più avrai accesso al **Forum** della community, dove poter chiarire tutti i tuoi dubbi e fare domande a cui risponderà anche Joe in persona, a un corso di **Business English**, **Phrase Book** e i migliori video YouTube di Joe!

Vai su

www.JoEnglish.com

e attiva subito un account per perfezionare ed allenare il tuo inglese

Part 1: Multiple choice

B2 First Listening

Prepare

This first part of the B2 First Listening examination consists of eight short extracts, which could be monologues or dialogues. Each extract has one multiple-choice question with three options: A, B or C. There is one mark for each correct answer. You will listen to each extract **twice**. These questions test your ability to:

- understand the topic or the purpose of the extract
- identify the overall meaning of the extract or specific details
- identify how speakers feel or their attitude towards a topic or situation
- understand when two speakers agree or disagree.

Suggestions to help you do well in this task

Before you listen

- Read the questions carefully. They will tell you the contexts of the listening extracts and what information you are listening for.
- While reading the options, think about synonyms for the main words/verbs. Don't 'word match'! If you hear the exact same word in the audio as in one of the options, it's probably not the correct answer, it's a **distractor**.
- Be prepared to hear some or all the options, either directly or indirectly.

While you listen

- When doing this part of the listening examination, there are different listening techniques you can use. Remember, you can listen twice!
- Technique 1: The first time you listen, close your eyes and forget about the questions; just concentrate on understanding as much as possible. Then, during the second time you listen, having already listened once you can focus on the question and answer.
- Technique 2: The first time you listen, try to answer the question. Then, when you listen for a second time you can concentrate on checking your answer.
- It's important to practise this in order to find which technique works best for you.

Have a go at some practice questions on the following pages.

Practise 1

You are going to hear two listening extracts. **Before** you listen to the audio, read the questions below and underline the key words in the questions and options.

Ask yourself:

- How are the questions and options in Questions 1 and 2 different?
- Can you think of any other ways of saying these options?

1. You hear two friends talking about going to a theme park. What is the woman annoyed about?

    A   the prices
    B   the rides
    C   the queues

2. You hear a man talking about traffic in the city. He thinks that the council should:

    A   extend the area covered by public transport.
    B   charge car drivers to enter the city centre.
    C   limit the city centre to pedestrians only.

Practise 2

Now listen to the audio and read the extracts for Questions 1 and 2. Select the correct answer A, B or C. Then:

- highlight the part of the extract where you identified the answer
- underline parts of the extracts connected to the distracting options.

Extract 1	

Man	You went to Splash World at the weekend, didn't you? Did you have a good time? My kids love it there.
Woman	We normally love a theme park too, but it could have been better to be honest. We decided to go as it's low season and we thought the queues would be smaller. Well, that was true, but only half the rides were working! The ones my eldest wanted to go on were all under maintenance.
Man	Really? You'd think they'd reduce the ticket prices for that!
Woman	Well, any theme park is pretty expensive these days. We still made the best of it.

B2 Listening | Part 1: Multiple choice

Extract 2

The council really needs to take action on the traffic – it's awful these days. I know some city councils have introduced those systems where people pay if they're coming into the city centre, but I'm not sure that would work personally. I'd rather have a completely traffic-free zone, even for the buses. I don't see why the council can't make this happen. Especially as it's cheap compared to other options. The issue for me, of course, is that I can't get a bus from where I live. It's about five kilometres from the city, but I tend to cycle most places so it's not a big problem.

Practise 3

Now you are going to listen to four more extracts. For Questions 3–6, choose the correct answer A, B or C.

3. You hear part of a conversation between two friends. What are they talking about?

   A Moving house
   B A family celebration
   C Going on holiday

4. You hear a woman leaving an answerphone message. Why is she calling?

   A To confirm some details
   B To postpone something
   C To ask for assistance

5. You hear two people discussing what they did at the weekend. What do they both say about the campsite?

   A The management was impressive.
   B The setting was picturesque.
   C The facilities were adequate.

6. You hear two people talking about a concert. They agree that:

   A the sound quality was poor.
   B the venue was too crowded.
   C the band were disappointing.

Answers and transcripts on pages 162–165

Put it to the test 1

 1_T_1

You will hear people talking in eight different situations. For Questions 1–8, choose the correct answer, A, B or C.

1. You hear two parents talking about their children's football match. How does the woman feel about the match?

   A   The final result was unfair.
   B   One team played badly.
   C   It was an exciting match.

2. You hear a news story on local radio. What is the purpose of the announcement?

   A   To promote an event
   B   To recommend an activity
   C   To support a proposal

3. You hear part of a conversation between a customer and a tourist office assistant. What does the woman want to know about?

   A   Train times
   B   Airport transfers
   C   Bus tours

4. You hear a station announcement about a delayed train. Passengers who want to go to Manchester should:

   A   wait for information.
   B   buy a new ticket.
   C   take another train.

5. You hear two friends talking about booking tickets. They agree to:

   A   wait until later.
   B   get them in person.
   C   sit separately.

6. You hear a gardener talking about his work. What does he dislike about his job?

   A   The salary is quite low.
   B   The work is unpredictable.
   C   The schedule is exhausting.

7. You hear two friends talking about online shopping. What annoys the man?

   A Poor products
   B Slow payment
   C Delivery charges

8. You hear a teacher talking to her students. What is she telling them about?

   A Changes to exam dates.
   B Arrangements for a trip.
   C An important email.

Watch out for **distractors** – information that may lead to choosing a wrong answer!

Put it to the test 2

 1_T_2

You will hear people talking in eight different situations. For Questions 1–8, choose the correct answer, A, B or C.

1. You hear two people talking about an art exhibition. What do they agree about?

   A The artist was brilliant.
   B It needed more artworks.
   C The works were confusing.

2. You hear two people talking about buying a new car. What is important for the woman?

   A Brand
   B Size
   C Cost

3. You hear a tour guide talking about a city. Why does he recommend the old town?

   A To hear traditional music.
   B To eat cheaply.
   C To see great architecture.

Answers and transcripts on pages 165–172

4. You hear part of an interview with an actor. How did he get started in his career?

   A   He met a director by chance.
   B   He was hired by an agency.
   C   He applied for a lot of roles.

5. You will hear a man leaving an answerphone message. What is the main reason for his message?

   A   To promise something
   B   To blame someone
   C   To praise somewhere

6. You hear two people talking about changes in their town. What does the woman think about the art gallery?

   A   It is a positive addition to the town.
   B   It will be welcomed by residents.
   C   It has changed the look of the town.

7. You hear two people talking about a trip. What are they discussing?

   A   The transport
   B   The accommodation
   C   The day trips

8. You hear a student talking about finishing her university course. How does she feel about the experience?

   A   It made her more realistic.
   B   It was too competitive.
   C   It changed her work goals.

Part 2: Sentence completion

B2 First Listening

Prepare

The second part of the B2 First Listening examination consists of one longer extract of 3–4 minutes, which is a monologue. You must complete ten sentences about this extract. Complete the gaps with words you hear on the recording. There is one mark for each correct answer. You will listen to each extract **twice**. These questions test your ability to:

- understand detail
- identify specific information
- identify the speaker's opinion
- follow longer speech.

Suggestions to help you do well in this task

Before you listen

- Read the sentences carefully. They will tell you the context of the listening extract and what information you are listening for. You will have 45 seconds before the audio starts, so use this time wisely.
- Underline key words in the sentence. This will help you identify a correct answer.
- Focus on the gaps. Look at the grammar of the sentence and try to identify what kind of word can complete the gap (e.g. noun, verb or adjective). Many are nouns.
- Think of possible answers to complete the gap. What answers would make sense in the sentence?

While you listen

- Note down the answers you think complete the gaps. Only use words you hear. **Do not** change any words.
- Use the underlined key words to keep moving through the questions. If you find one question very hard, or do not hear the answer, leave it and move on. Remember, you will hear the extract twice.
- You might hear some distracting information. Remember that the words must match grammatically and agree with **all** the information in the sentence.
- Don't write too much. Answers will be no more than three words in length.

Have a go at some practice questions on the following pages.

Practise 1

You are going to hear a man called Nick talking about training to be a chef. **Before** you listen to the audio, read the sentences (1–4) below and underline the key words.

Ask yourself:

- What kind of words need to go into the gaps?
- What clues in the sentences help you know what kind of word completes the gaps?
- What words seem possible or likely?

Nick was originally interested in being a **(1)** ___Lawyer___ .   noun – job: doctor, teacher, police officer?

While he was at university, Nick worked at a **(2)**_____.

Nick's **(3)**_____ were pleased that he decided to be a chef.

Doing a college course gave Nick some **(4)**_____ for cookery.

Practise 2

Now listen to the audio and read the following extract for sentences 1–4. Complete the sentences with a word or short phrase. Then:

- highlight the part of the extract where you identified the answer
- underline parts of the extract connected to the distracting options.

Extract 1

Hello. My name is Nick, and I'm going to tell you all about what it takes to be a chef. Now, I didn't always want to be a chef, but I was always interested in food. You see, my dad is a farmer and I grew up helping out a lot. But actually I wanted to be a lawyer. It sounded much more exciting!

It all changed when I went to university, though, and I started cooking my own food. I found that more interesting than my degree course. I used to study during the day and then get cooking books out of the library to find out more about it. I did all that while helping out at a bike shop… and I spent everything that I made there on trying new foods.

I decided at the end of my degree that I wanted to be a chef. It was a bit of a shock for my parents, who thought I had wasted my time at university, but my housemates were really

supportive of me. But they had tasted the food I'd learnt to cook, and they knew I had talent.

So, I started looking for training courses. I could have done another degree, but I wanted practical experience in a kitchen. I ended up doing a part-time course and also working as an apprentice chef part-time too. I picked up lots of basic skills on the course, like working with meat and how to store foods, and I learnt creativity and speed in the restaurant.

Practise 3

Now you are going to listen to the rest of the extract. For Sentences 5–10, complete the sentences with a word or short phrase.

Nick thinks that the **(5)**_____ is the hardest thing about being a chef.

At first, Nick couldn't add much **(6)**_____ to his dishes.

Nick thinks the best dish on the menu is the **(7)**_____.

Nick tries to avoid making **(8)**_____ if he can.

The approach of **(9)**_____ makes Nick's restaurant different from others.

Nick recommends gaining some **(10)**_____ as a first step into being a chef.

Answers and transcripts on pages 172–174

Put it to the test 1

 2_T_1

You will hear a woman called Grace from the tourist office talking about a Scottish Island. For Questions 1–10, complete the sentences with a word or short phrase.

Grace thinks the best thing about the island is the **(1)**_____.

Visitors can often view different types of **(2)**_____ from the boat.

After some people going to **(3)**_____ stopped at the island, it became famous.

(4)_____ are too large to get into the cave.

Its alternative name probably comes from a visit by a **(5)**_____.

The **(6)**_____ caused the only people living on the island to leave.

The only building on the island is a **(7)**_____.

The island is now owned by a **(8)**_____.

You can walk up to the **(9)**_____ during the tours.

It's a good idea to look at the **(10)**_____ before going on a tour.

B2 Listening | Part 2: Sentence completion

Put it to the test 2

 2_T_2

You will hear a man called Martin Jackson talking about a community garden he helped to create. For Questions 1–10, complete the sentences with a word or short phrase.

The residents in Martin's block of flats wanted the garden to be used for (1)_____.

Adding some (2)_____ will make the community garden brighter and more attractive.

The residents (3)_____ the various jobs that need doing in the garden.

Martin was surprised that he needed a lot of (4)_____ to do the spraying.

The covered (5)_____ means that people can be in the garden all year round.

Martin noticed that residents (6)_____ differently because of the garden.

Community gardens in cities highlight the importance of (7)_____ and connection.

It is common to see gardens on (8)_____ and public buildings.

Martin points out that the roofs of city buildings are often (9)_____.

The residents might invest in (10)_____ so they can use rainwater in the garden.

Answers and transcripts on pages 174–176

Part 3: Multiple matching

B2 First Listening

Prepare

Part 3 of the B2 First Listening examination consists of five short monologues, each lasting about 30 seconds. All the speakers will talk about the same topic but from a different point of view. You have to match what each speaker says to a list of options. There are eight options so three are not needed. There is one mark for each correct answer. You will listen to each extract **twice**. These questions test your ability to:

- understand detail
- identify specific information
- understand different speakers
- identify different opinions and feelings.

Suggestions to help you do well in this task

Before you listen

- Read the instructions carefully. They will tell you the general topic of the monologues **and** what kind of information you are listening for.
- Underline the topic and the question or specific information you need to focus on.
- Underline key words in the options. Notice how the options are different and what specific details are presented in each of the options.
- You will have 30 seconds before the audio starts, so use this time wisely by thinking about what synonyms you might hear on the recording.

While you listen

- Wait until the end of each monologue before you choose your answer. The speakers will mention some of the key words in more than one of the options, but only one option will match **exactly**.
- Remember that you will hear the extract twice, so as you listen for the first time make a note of the possible answers.
- When you listen for the second time, choose the answer you are most sure about.
- Listen for synonyms and different ways to say the information in the options.

Have a go at some practice questions on the following pages.

Practise 1

Before you listen to the audio, read the instructions and options below. Underline the question in the instruction and the key words in the options.

Ask yourself:

- What does the question focus on?
- Can you think of any other ways to say the options?

Next, you will hear two short extracts in which people are talking about practising a sport. For Questions 1 and 2, choose from the list (A–H), the main goal of each speaker. Use the letters only once. There are three extra letters that you do not need to use.

A to train with other people more
B to increase their physical strength
C to become more sociable
D to strengthen their determination
E to implement a routine
F to win a competition
G to improve a specific technique
H to manage stress from work

Speaker 1: [1]
Speaker 2: [2]

Practise 2

 3_P_2

Now listen to the audio and read the following extracts for Questions 1 and 2. Choose from the list (A–H) the main goal of each speaker. Then:

- highlight the part of the extract where you identified the answer
- underline parts of the extracts connected to the distracting options.

Extract 1

I'm training for a marathon next year. I don't think it will be too difficult because I've run some 10K races before. I'm quite self-motivated and have created my own schedule: I run three times a week before work and then once at the weekend with my running club. But the thing I'm a little bit concerned about is whether I'm strong enough. I'm going to need to spend a lot more time in the gym doing weights and exercises to build up my leg muscles. At the moment they're good for short distances, but I have to change this if I want to actually finish a marathon.

Extract 2

I took up yoga last year because I work long hours at a computer and was suffering from hip pain. At first, I found it hard to build time for yoga into my daily life. I was always distracted by something. I decided to join a class, which gave me some structure, and the classes started to make a difference – and now I feel more motivated to do it at home. I aim to plan my home yoga sessions at the beginning of each week and make sure that nothing gets in the way. I've got quite a busy and stressful life, but I'm sure I can devote time to it.

Practise 3

🎧 3_P_3

Now, you will hear the final three speakers. For Questions 3–5, choose from the list (A–H) the main goal of each speaker.

- **A** to train with other people more
- **B** to increase their physical strength
- **C** to become more sociable
- **D** to strengthen their determination
- **E** to implement a routine
- **F** to win a competition
- **G** to improve a specific technique
- **H** to manage stress from work

Speaker 3: | 3 |
Speaker 4: | 4 |
Speaker 5: | 5 |

Answers and transcripts on pages 178–180

JoEnglish Let's Go Cambridge! B2 First Reading and Listening

Put it to the test 1

 3_T_1

You will hear five short extracts in which people talking about travelling by plane. For Questions 1–5, choose from the list (A–H) what each person feels about it. Use the letters only once. There are three extra letters that you do not need to use.

A   Thinks it's too complicated

B   Enjoys the sense of adventure

C   Makes them feel nervous

D   Prefers flying alone

E   Finds it uncomfortable

F   Likes the service

G   Enjoys the luxury

H   Likes looking out the window

Speaker 1: [1]
Speaker 2: [2]
Speaker 3: [3]
Speaker 4: [4]
Speaker 5: [5]

Put it to the test 2

 3_T_2

You will hear five short extracts in which people talking about their first day at school. For Questions 1–5, choose from the list (A–H) each person's strongest memory. Use the letters only once. There are three extra letters that you do not need to use.

A   The worry of being a new student

B   The assistance from the staff

C   The design of the building

D   The excitement of making friends

E   The personality of their teacher

F   The equipment in their classroom

G   The number of people

H   The range of fun activities

Speaker 1: [1]
Speaker 2: [2]
Speaker 3: [3]
Speaker 4: [4]
Speaker 5: [5]

Answers and transcripts on pages 181–183

Part 4: Multiple choice

B2 First Listening

Prepare

The final part of the B2 First Listening examination consists of one longer extract of 3–4 minutes, which is a dialogue between two speakers. There are seven multiple-choice questions about the extract. These will follow the order of the information you hear. The questions each have three options: A, B or C. There is one mark for each correct answer. You will listen to each extract **twice**. These questions test your ability to:

- understand main ideas and identify specific information
- identify the speaker's opinion and attitude
- follow longer speech.

Suggestions to help you do well in this task

Before you listen

- Read all the questions. They will tell you the context of the listening extract, what kind of information you are listening for and how the conversation will develop.
- Underline key words in the questions. Think of possible synonyms.
- Focus on the options. When you read the options, underline the key words and notice the differences between each option.
- Be prepared to hear some or all the options, either directly or indirectly. But remember that only one option answers the question correctly.

While you listen

- Choose the option (A, B or C) that you think is correct. Check your answer by trying to rule out the other two options. Remember (see page 105), you can listen twice!
- If you find one question hard, don't spend too much time thinking about it. Remember to move on to the next question as the subject changes.
- Try to 'guess' the answer. That sounds strange, but it can focus your listening so that you can determine whether that answer is correct or not. Any extra focus is important!
- Don't be distracted by the other answer options. Remember, extracts will contain **distractors**.

Have a go at some practice questions on the following pages.

Practise 1

You will hear an interview with Alex Blakely, who manages a summer camp, talking about the benefits for teenagers.

Before you listen to the audio, read Questions 1–3 and underline the key words:

1. Alex believes summer camps are a good experience because:

    A they only last a short time.
    B the staff are well qualified.
    C there is a range of activities on offer.

2. How are summer camps different from school?

    A They have more activities.
    B They are more flexible.
    C They focus more on skills.

3. What does Alex say teenagers develop on the camp?

    A Leadership skills
    B Independence
    C Self confidence

Now tick (✓) the points in the list (A–F) that you think will be included in the interview. Which parts of the questions helped you decide?

    A Things that teenagers learn on summer camps   ☐
    B A description of different types of summer camp   ☐
    C Why teenagers prefer summer camps to school   ☐
    D How to help teenagers who get homesick   ☐
    E A comparison with school activities   ☐
    F Advantages of attending a summer camp   ☐

Practise 2

 4_P_2

Now listen to the audio and read the extract for Questions 1–3. Choose the correct answer and then:

- highlight the part of the extract where you identified the answer
- underline parts of the extract connected to the distracting options.

B2 Listening | Part 4: Multiple choice

Extract 1

Interviewer   I'm joined this morning by Alex Blakely, manager of the UK's largest summer camp. He believes that all parents should seriously consider sending their teenagers on a summer camp. So, tell us Alex, why are you convinced that this is such as great idea?

Alex   Hello. Well, for me it's about opening their eyes to new things. In their daily lives, teenagers might go to a dance class or play a sport, or attend a weekly group like Scouts. But here they're able to try out so many things they've never done before. Our staff have a lot of experience working with young people, and we really want them to make the most of their time with us. After all, most participants only spend two or three weeks at camp.

Interviewer   Some parents don't want to pay for an experience that they feel is similar to school. What is your opinion on this?

Alex   Even though the teenagers are a similar age, and the activities are all learning experiences, summer camps are unique. This is because there is a lot more freedom. We don't have a prescribed programme. Also, we encourage participants to get involved with as many or as few activities as they want.

Interviewer   What skills do teenagers learn at the camp?

Alex   At this age, young people are developing their identity quite rapidly. We're keen to show them ways to do this successfully. Although they cannot be fully in charge of their day-to-day lives, we want them to grow as people. Positive learning experiences at the camp make students see their abilities more clearly.

Practise 3

Now you are going to listen to the rest of the extract. For Questions 4–7, choose the best answer (A, B or C).

4. What do the camp counsellors help teenagers do?

     A   Solve friendship issues

     B   Be more emotional

     C   Learn how to argue

5. Why are teenagers not allowed mobile phones at the camp?

     A   To help them rely on technology less

     B   To prevent contact with their parents

     C   To improve communication skills

Answers and transcripts on pages 184–185

6. When choosing a summer camp, parents prefer places that:

   A are convenient to get to.

   B offer water sports.

   C other parents recommend.

7. After summer camp, parents often report that their children:

   A keep the house tidier.

   B get up earlier in the morning.

   C organise themselves better.

> Watch out for **distractors** – information that may lead to choosing a wrong answer!

Put it to the test 1

You will hear part of an interview with Victoria Bradshaw, who works as a vet, talking about the challenges and rewards of her job. For Questions 1–7, choose the best answer (A, B or C).

1. What does Victoria say about studying to be a vet?

   A It was harder than she expected.

   B She adapted to the course demands.

   C It was a rewarding experience.

2. According to Victoria, team meetings help the vets:

   A deal with stressful situations.

   B make decisions more quickly.

   C come up with new approaches.

3. Why is talking to pet owners difficult for vets?

   A They are very emotional.

   B They can be unpredictable.

   C They want positive news.

Answers and transcripts on pages 185–186

B2 Listening | Part 4: Multiple choice

4. Working as a farm vet helped Victoria to:

   A   rely on her knowledge.
   B   improve her communication.
   C   manage her schedule.

5. What did Victoria admire about farmers?

   A   Their approach to animals' health issues.
   B   The way they communicate with vets.
   C   How they care for their animals.

6. Victoria thinks that managing a veterinary practice:

   A   is something she would like to do one day.
   B   could become boring after a while.
   C   would not be the best use of her skills.

7. How has technology affected Victoria's job?

   A   The paperwork has been reduced.
   B   The practice has more customers.
   C   The staff have become more efficient.

Put it to the test 2

 4_T_2

You will hear part of an interview with Tom Lawrence, a chess player. For Questions 1–7, choose the best answer (A, B or C).

1. Tom started playing chess because:

   A   he liked intellectual games.
   B   he wanted to please his parents.
   C   he had friends in a local club.

2. The thing that most interests Tom about chess is that:

   A   it involves a lot of luck.
   B   there are many strategies.
   C   each game is unique.

Answers and transcripts on pages 187–189

3. What do chess players begin to understand as they improve their skills?

   A That it's more difficult than it appears
   B That the rules are complicated
   C That losing is good for learning

4. What are the benefits of playing chess for the brain?

   A Improved intelligence
   B Better overall function
   C More creative thinking

5. What does Tom say about chess books?

   A They help beginners get started.
   B They are not worth the money.
   C They are useful for advanced players.

6. Tom thinks that chess remains popular because:

   A people of different ages like playing it.
   B there are so many opportunities to play it.
   C it is part of many cultures around the world.

7. What is Tom's assessment of playing chess against a computer?

   A It prepares players for competitions.
   B It provides limited practice.
   C It gives a wide range of practice.

Answers and transcripts on pages 189–191

Practice tests

Test 1 | pages 129–136

Part 1 *130*
Part 2 *132*
Part 3 *133*
Part 4 *134*

Test 2 | pages 137–144

Part 1 *138*
Part 2 *140*
Part 3 *141*
Part 4 *142*

Test 3 | pages 145–152

Part 1 *146*
Part 2 *148*
Part 3 *149*
Part 4 *150*

Test 4 | pages 153–160

Part 1 *154*
Part 2 *156*
Part 3 *157*
Part 4 *158*

Cambridge B2 First Listening

Practice test 1

Part 1

You will hear people talking in eight different situations. For Questions 1–8, choose the correct answer, A, B or C.

1. You hear a teacher talking to a parent about their daughter's behaviour. What negative point does the teacher mention?

   A   She doesn't listen to instructions.
   B   She distracts other children.
   C   She doesn't work well in groups.

2. You hear two friends talking about a hotel they stayed at recently. What did they both enjoy about it?

   A   the range of food and drinks
   B   the location of the hotel
   C   the service from the staff

3. You hear a man talking about his hobby of growing tomatoes. What is he talking about?

   A   caring for the plants
   B   when to plant the seeds
   C   good soil for tomatoes

4. You hear a woman talking about wind farms. She thinks that the local government should:

   A   stop building them near houses.
   B   replace them with solar power.
   C   spend less money on them.

Transcripts on pages 195–197

5. You hear a shop assistant talking to a customer.
   What is the man's opinion of the jacket?

   A It's not his style.
   B It's over his budget.
   C It's the wrong colour.

6. You hear part of a news programme on the radio.
   Where will the new shopping centre be built?

   A behind the train station
   B on the edge of the town
   C next to the business district

7. You hear two friends talking about getting fit.
   The woman is optimistic that she will:

   A lose weight.
   B become stronger.
   C run faster.

8. You hear two friends talking about being members of a book club.
   Why did he join the book club?

   A to get inspiration
   B to discuss books
   C to meet new people

Part 2

You will hear a tour guide talking about London Bridge to some visitors. For questions 9–18, complete the sentences with a word or short phrase.

Britain sold London Bridge because of problems with the **(9)**_____.

The previous bridge was too **(10)**_____ and had to be replaced.

The move of the bridge was completed in the **(11)**_____.

McCulloch's aim was for **(12)**_____ to buy property in the area.

Now, the inside of the bridge is made of **(13)**_____.

The bridge was initially rebuilt over **(14)**_____ when it came to Arizona.

The lights on the bridge change for **(15)**_____.

There are more **(16)**_____ than any other animal living on the bridge.

The **(17)**_____ mean that the bridge will last for many years.

The tour guide recommends the **(18)**_____ after the tour.

Transcripts on pages 197–198

B2 Listening | Practice test 1

 P_1_3

Part 3

You will hear five short extracts in which people are talking about moving from the city to the countryside. For questions 19–23, choose from the list (A–H) what each person feels about it. Use the letters only once. There are three extra letters which you do not need to use.

A   It can be inconvenient.

B   There is a sense of community.

C   Entertainment could be improved.

D   Public transport is terrible.

E   Local shopkeepers are friendly.

F   The cost of living is lower.

G   More businesses are needed.

H   The quality of life is good.

Speaker 1: 19
Speaker 2: 20
Speaker 3: 21
Speaker 4: 22
Speaker 5: 23

Answers on page 192

JoEnglish Let's Go Cambridge! B2 First Reading and Listening

🎧 P_1_4

Part 4

You will hear part of a radio interview with Emily Jones, who is talking about the natural skincare products she makes. For Questions 24–30, choose the best answer (A, B or C).

---

24. Emily started making her own skincare products because:

    A she was interested in plants.

    B she needed to increase her income.

    C her son had skin problems.

25. What was difficult for Emily when she started her business?

    A marketing her products

    B finding time for research

    C getting customer feedback

26. Where did Emily find help to grow her business?

    A her previous manager

    B an online forum

    C a local business group

27. What does Emily enjoy about her job?

    A completing legal documents

    B responding to customer complaints

    C writing product descriptions

Transcripts on pages 199–200

28. Emily would advise small business owners to:

A find a good accountant.
B ask friends and family for help.
C pay for a professional website.

29. According to Emily, people buy her products because they:

A are good value for money.
B are based on science.
C use fewer chemicals.

30. Emily thinks that future skincare products will:

A use sustainable packaging.
B contain a lot of vitamins.
C use organic ingredients.

Answers on page 192

Cambridge B2 First Listening

Practice test 2

Part 1

You will hear people talking in eight different situations. For Questions 1–8, choose the correct answer, A, B or C.

1. You hear part of a conversation between two colleagues. What are they talking about?

    A a conference
    B a training course
    C a presentation

2. You hear an announcement at a sports match. What should families do?

    A wait to leave the stadium
    B ask for assistance
    C go out the West exit

3. You hear part of a conversation between a shop assistant and a customer. What is the problem with the phone?

    A it's got a poor battery
    B the screen is dark
    C it gets too hot

4. You hear two friends talking about their recent holiday. They agree that the:

    A resort was unpleasant.
    B weather was changeable.
    C hotel was disappointing.

Transcripts on pages 201–203

5. You hear a woman talking about a film she saw. Why did she watch the film?

   A   because she'd read about it
   B   because someone recommended it
   C   because she's a fan of the director

6. You hear a policeman talking about his job. What does he think about his job?

   A   It's harder than he thought.
   B   It's different to what people think.
   C   It's more boring than he expected.

7. You hear a woman talking about driving. What annoys the woman?

   A   slow drivers
   B   strong headlights
   C   bad parking

8. You hear an advertisement on the radio. What is it for?

   A   a hair salon
   B   a wedding planner
   C   a cleaning service

Part 2

You will hear a man called Hugo talking to a group of local people about road safety. For questions 9–18, complete the sentences with a word or short phrase.

The talk is focused on the safety of **(9)**_____.

Hugo will use information from some **(10)**_____ in the talk.

Failure to use a **(11)**_____ makes accidents more likely to occur.

People should wait to establish **(12)**_____ before walking across a road.

(13)_____ is recommended for people walking in the evenings.

Most accidents are caused by **(14)**_____.

The council has begun **(15)**_____ to improve the safety of walkers.

Hugo believes flashing road signs will be **(16)**_____.

The **(17)**_____ is a new road-safety technology we can use now.

The **(18)**_____ is keen on the development of artificial intelligence (AI) technologies.

Transcripts on pages 203–204

B2 Listening | Practice test 2

Part 3

You will hear five short extracts in which people are talking about an art course. For questions 19–23, choose from the list (A–H) why they decided to take the course. Use the letters only once. There are three extra letters which you do not need to use.

A   To help them relax.

B   To improve their ability.

C   To start a hobby.

D   To meet new people.

E   To complete a project.

F   To improve their opportunities.

G   To try something different.

H   To give them more confidence.

Speaker 1: [19]
Speaker 2: [20]
Speaker 3: [21]
Speaker 4: [22]
Speaker 5: [23]

Answers on page 193

Part 4

You will hear part of an interview with Chris Walker and Louise Franklin talking about what it's like to work as rock-climbing instructors. For Questions 24–30, choose the best answer (A, B or C).

24. Louise became interested in rock climbing after:

   A watching a documentary.
   B reading a book.
   C talking to a friend.

25. What made Chris and Louise decide to become instructors?

   A a bad experience on a course
   B joining a climbing club
   C watching other instructors

26. In order to become an instructor, it is necessary to:

   A have experience.
   B complete six courses.
   C pass an exam.

27. The instructor course highlighted that Chris needed to:

   A work on his physical condition.
   B improve his communication skills.
   C listen to instructions carefully.

Transcripts on pages 205–206

28. According to Louise, rock climbing is:

   A   accessible to everyone.
   B   a good personal challenge.
   C   not as difficult as it looks.

29. What should people new to rock climbing bear in mind?

   A   Don't be afraid of falling.
   B   Don't give up too quickly.
   C   Don't pay a lot for a course.

30. How has rock climbing affected Chris?

   A   He is more connected to nature.
   B   He has increased his self-confidence.
   C   He feels more satisfied with life.

Cambridge B2 First Listening

Practice test 3

Part 1

You will hear people talking in eight different situations. For Questions 1–8, choose the correct answer, A, B or C.

1. You hear an answerphone message. Why is the woman calling?

   A   to ask for some advice
   B   to change some plans
   C   to give some information

2. You hear part of a conversation about buying a house.
   Why does the man want a house with a garden?

   A   so his children can play outside.
   B   because he enjoys barbecues.
   C   so his dog has space to run around.

3. You hear a tour guide talking to a group of tourists.
   When was the original castle built?

   A   17th Century
   B   18th Century
   C   19th Century

4. You hear two friends making travel plans. Wgat does the man **not** want to do?

   A   get up early
   B   go by bus
   C   pay for a seat

Transcripts on pages 207–208

5. You hear two friends talking about their work. What are they talking about?

   A a presentation
   B a project
   C an event

6. You hear two parents discussing dinner.
   What do they decide to do on Saturday night?

   A get a delivery
   B go to a restaurant
   C cook at home

7. You hear two friends arranging a day out together. What do they agree to go to?

   A a flower show
   B a play
   C a festival

8. You hear a teacher talking about mobile phones in the classroom.
   What does he think about them?

   A They should not be allowed in class.
   B They stop students concentrating.
   C They are a useful tool for teachers.

Answers on page 193

Part 2

You will hear a woman called Paula talking about developing video games. For questions 9–18, complete the sentences with a word or short phrase.

Most people play video games to gain a feeling of **(9)**_____.

One advantage of gaming is that it's an escape from **(10)**_____.

Paula works in the **(11)**_____.

The way the game looks often depends on what the **(12)**_____ is like.

Management gives the team a **(13)**_____ and deadline.

Paula describes the process of development as a **(14)**_____.

Most of their advertising is done through **(15)**_____.

They offer support in many different **(16)**_____.

They normally find a few **(17)**_____ after the game has been released.

Some people in the video game industry are **(18)**_____.

Transcripts on pages 209–211

B2 Listening | Practice test 3

 P_3_3

Part 3

You will hear five short extracts in which people are talking about working with children. For questions 19–23, choose from the list (A–H) what each person enjoys about it. Use the letters only once. There are three extra letters which you do not need to use.

A Seeing their personalities develop.

B Learning about child psychology.

C Seeing how creative they can be.

D Discovering what they like to do.

E Helping them solve problems.

F Telling parents about their progress.

G Researching new teaching techniques.

H Watching them become more confident.

Speaker 1: 19
Speaker 2: 20
Speaker 3: 21
Speaker 4: 22
Speaker 5: 23

Answers on pages 193–194

151

Part 4

You will hear a radio interview with a woman called Natasha Evans talking about what it's like to be the manager of a sports shop. For Questions 24–30, choose the best answer (A, B or C).

24. What does Natasha say is an important part of her job?

   A finding interesting new products
   B keeping up to date with sports news
   C watching different types of sports

25. What are young people most interested in buying?

   A designer trainers
   B football shirts
   C famous brands

26. According to Natasha, her success is a result of:

   A spending time with customers.
   B offering a range of products.
   C giving good discounts.

27. What aspect of the clothing and sportswear business is Natasha currently studying?

   A sustainable fashion
   B consumer behaviour
   C factory working conditions

Transcripts on pages 211–212

28. Natasha encourages her employees to:

   A   contribute their ideas.

   B   get more qualifications.

   C   attend industry events.

29. Natasha admits that she isn't always good at:

   A   using technology at work.

   B   having enough items in stock.

   C   preparing for surprises.

30. What does Natasha say is happening in her industry?

   A   attitudes to casual clothing are changing

   B   brands are producing higher quality clothing

   C   people want more choice in sportswear

Cambridge B2 First Listening

Practice test 4

JoEnglish Let's Go Cambridge! B2 First Reading and Listening

🎧 P_4_1

Part 1

You will hear people talking in eight different situations. For Questions 1–8, choose the correct answer, A, B or C.

1. You hear two people discussing a problem. What do they agree to do?

   A   see a mechanic
   B   ignore the problem
   C   check the internet

2. You hear a woman talking about her first job. What was her first job?

   A   receptionist
   B   nurse
   C   doctor

3. You hear a man talking on the radio about fishing.
   The official reason for the fishing fines is:

   A   to maintain fish supplies.
   B   to keep fishermen safe.
   C   to promote the local area.

4. You hear an interview with a football manager. What does she find most exciting?

   A   the time before the game
   B   seeing the players improve
   C   watching the game develop

Transcripts on pages 213–214

5. You hear two friends having an argument. What did the man do wrong?

   A he forgot something
   B he took something
   C he lost something

6. You hear a writer talking about her new book. What is she doing?

   A explaining where she got her ideas from
   B outlining the difficulty of being a writer
   C justifying the way she wrote the book

7. You hear a man talking about a concert he went to. How does he feel about it?

   A impressed by the musicians
   B annoyed it was so uncomfortable
   C pleased that he got tickets

8. You hear two friends talking about a new shop. What did they both dislike about it?

   A the clothes are expensive
   B the staff is unpleasant
   C the design is old-fashioned

Part 2

You will hear David, who is an adventurer, talking about going inside a volcano. For questions 9–18, complete the sentences with a word or short phrase.

David was **(9)**_____ to go into a volcano.

David had a difficult walk to the **(10)**_____.

It's possible to get a **(11)**_____ directly to the mouth of the volcano.

David was surprised by the **(12)**_____ on his way to the volcano.

The guides gave a **(13)**_____ which David thought was essential.

David compares the lift to the type that **(14)**_____ use.

People who go inside the volcano might be worried about the **(15)**_____ as you enter.

Once inside the volcano, they had to remain on the **(16)**_____.

When they returned to the top, David had some **(17)**_____.

The emptiness of the volcano is a **(18)**_____.

Transcripts on pages 215–217

B2 Listening | Practice test 4

Part 3

You will hear five short extracts in which people are talking about how they help to protect the environment. For questions 19–23, choose from the list (A–H) why each person does it. Use the letters only once. There are three extra letters which you do not need to use.

A   For the future of the planet.

B   For their own children.

C   To make where they live nicer.

D   To set an example to others.

E   Because they are told to do it.

F   To stop waste.

G   Because it's the right thing to do.

H   To save wildlife in their area.

Speaker 1: 19
Speaker 2: 20
Speaker 3: 21
Speaker 4: 22
Speaker 5: 23

Answers on page 194

JoEnglish Let's Go Cambridge! B2 First Reading and Listening

P_4_4

Part 4

You will hear a radio interview with a psychologist called Rachel talking about why people enjoy theme parks. For Questions 24–30, choose the best answer (A, B or C).

24. When did Rachel get into the area of theme-park psychology?

　A　after realising it was a well-paid area
　B　after going to a famous theme park
　C　after seeing a talk at a conference

25. Why do families tend to go to theme parks?

　A　to create memories
　B　to prevent boredom
　C　to strengthen bonds

26. One study found that most people go on scary rides to:

　A　impress their friends.
　B　feel the excitement.
　C　experience stress.

27. What do people generally think about long waiting times?

　A　they make the ride more popular
　B　they build up the excitement
　C　they put people off visiting

Transcripts on pages 217–218

28. What does Rachel say about the colours of theme parks?

    A they are tailored to certain areas
    B they are bright and energetic throughout
    C they think about the customers' desires

29. How do theme parks encourage visitors to the shop?

    A by controlling the air-conditioning
    B by putting children's items at the front
    C by positioning them near exits

30. How does she summarise visiting a theme park?

    A the visitor uses all their senses
    B the visitor is never in control
    C the visitor is the priority

Answers on page 194

# Answers

Part 1: Multiple choice | pages 162–172

Practise 162
Put it to the test 1 165
Put it to the test 2 168

Part 2: Sentence matching | pages 172–178

Practise 172
Put it to the test 1 174
Put it to the test 2 176

Part 3: Multiple matching | pages 178–183

Practise 178
Put it to the test 1 181
Put it to the test 2 182

Part 4: Multiple choice | pages 184–191

Practise 184
Put it to the test 1 187
Put it to the test 2 189

JoEnglish Let's Go Cambridge! B2 First Reading and Listening

Part 1: Practise 1 | Answers   (page 106)

1. You hear two friends talking about going to a theme park. What is the woman annoyed about?

   A the prices
   B the rides
   C the queues

   Question 1 is a direct question. The options are all short.

   prices – money to get in, cost, entrance fee, pay, amount
   rides – attractions
   queues – waiting times, lines

2. You hear a man talking about traffic in the city. He thinks that the council should:

   A extend the area covered by public transport
   B charge car drivers to enter the city centre
   C limit the city centre to pedestrians only.

   extend – increase, spread, make bigger
   area – zone, space
   public transport – buses, trains, trams
   charge – ask for money, pay
   car drivers – motorists, vehicle owners
   limit – stop, reduce,
   pedestrians – people walking, people on foot

   Question 2 requires you to complete the sentence with an option. The options are all longer and parts of a complete sentence.

Part 1: Practise 2 | Answers   (pages 106–107)

1. You hear two friends talking about going to a theme park. What is the woman annoyed about?

   A the prices
   B the rides
   C the queues

Transcript

Man	You went to Splash World at the weekend, didn't you? Did you have a good time? My kids love it there.
Woman	We normally love a theme park too, but it could have been better to be honest. We decided to go as it's low season and we thought the queues would be smaller. Well, that was true, but only half the rides were working! The ones my eldest wanted to go on were all under maintenance.
Man	Really? You'd think they'd reduce the ticket prices for that!
Woman	Well, any theme park is pretty expensive these days. We still made the best of it.

2. You hear a man talking about traffic in the city. He thinks that the council should:

   A extend the area covered by public transport.

   B charge car drivers to enter the city centre.

   C limit the city centre to pedestrians only.

Transcript

The council really needs to take action on the traffic – it's awful these days. I know some city councils have introduced those systems where people pay if they're coming into the city centre, but I'm not sure that would work personally. I'd rather have a completely traffic-free zone, even for the buses. I don't see why the council can't make this happen. Especially as it's cheap compared to other options. The issue for me, of course, is that I can't get a bus from where I live. It's about five kilometres from the city, but I tend to cycle most places so it's not a big problem.

Part 1: Practise 3 | Answers (page 107)

3. You hear part of a conversation between two friends. What are they talking about?

   A Moving house

   B A family celebration

   C Going on holiday

Transcript

Woman	You know, I could really do with a holiday, but I don't think that'll happen any time soon.
Man	Oh, I know the feeling! But what's wrong?
Woman	I'm just so exhausted after all the preparations for our move. It's taken ages for all the paperwork to be completed, and this last week I've had to help the children pack up all their belongings.
Man	You know, moving is such a big life event for all the family that I'm not surprised you feel like you need a break. Hopefully you can celebrate when you've unpacked.

4. You hear a woman leaving an answerphone message. Why is she calling?

   A To confirm some details

   B To postpone something

   C To ask for assistance

JoEnglish Let's Go Cambridge! B2 First Reading and Listening

Transcript

Hi there, Tom. I hope you haven't left the house already. I just wanted to let you know that the match has been called off because Andy's broken down on the motorway and he's got all the equipment with him. He's called the mechanic for help, but who knows how long that will take, so, we've got nothing to play with! I'm sure everyone will be disappointed, but there's just nothing we can do. Hopefully, we'll be able to play at the same time tomorrow instead, as long as the pitch is free and it doesn't rain. Does tomorrow at ten thirty work for you?

5. You hear two people discussing what they did at the weekend. What do they both say about the campsite?

- **A** The management was impressive.
- **B** The setting was picturesque.
- **C** The facilities were adequate.

Transcript

Woman — Would you go back to that campsite, Tony?

Man — Oh, absolutely. I mean, it was worth it just for the sunsets over the hills. They've chosen a great spot there, although the showers would benefit from un upgrade.

Woman — I thought they were acceptable, but I would have preferred a tent closer to the toilets. It was a bit of a trek during the night! For me, what stood out was how well organised they are. I mean, all the codes and information were on the app.

Man — And the fact that there was someone at reception 24 hours was fantastic. Not every campsite is like that, you know.

6. You hear two people talking about a concert. They agree that:

- **A** the sound quality was poor.
- **B** the venue was too crowded.
- **C** the band were disappointing.

Transcript

Woman — So, what did you think of the concert? It was so hot in there, wasn't it?!

Man — Yeah, I know! I was surprised, really. I mean, it can't have been from all the people considering the place was only half full.

Woman — Well, I can see why that was. I mean, the group was an hour late and only played a couple of their most well-known songs.

Man	Yeah, it's a real shame – especially since the ticket prices weren't cheap – and I couldn't hear anything other than the lead guitar!
Woman	Really? Maybe that's because you were standing in front of that massive speaker! You should have moved somewhere else.
Man	Oh, I hadn't even realised that might be why!

Part 1: Put it to the test 1 | Answers   (pages 108–109)

1. You hear two parents talking about their children's football match. How does the woman feel about the match?

   A The final result was unfair.
   B One team played badly.
   C It was an exciting match.

Transcript

Woman	Well, I'm glad that's over.
Man	Me too. What a boring game! That second half was terrible. It was like most of the kids were just waiting for the final whistle to blow.
Woman	Probably because of the rain! That usually makes everyone lose a bit of motivation. Still, I don't think the other team deserved to win really.
Man	Why not? I thought they played pretty well.
Woman	Oh yes, I'm not saying that. I just think so did my son's team – and we had more chances – but that's life, I suppose.

2. You hear a news story on local radio. What is the purpose of the announcement?

   A To promote an event
   B To recommend an activity
   C To support a proposal

Transcript

And in local news, the mayor's office has just announced that the new leisure centre will be officially opened in May, just in time for summer. This will be welcome news for all parents out there who've suffered two summers without any swimming facilities in the town. As well as two pools, the leisure centre includes tennis courts and a number of pitches for football and other sports. The mayor herself will attend the opening, and there will be music from local bands and a chance for people to take a look around. Entry will be free all day for residents to go and see what they think.

3. You hear part of a conversation between a customer and a tourist office assistant. What does the woman want to know about?

   A   Train times
   B   Airport transfers
   C   Bus tours

Transcript

Woman	Hi again! I hope you remember me!
Man	Yes, I do! How was the tour? I hope you enjoyed it!
Woman	I had a great time, but it rained a bit, so the open-top bus wasn't ideal. Thanks so much for your recommendation, though. In fact, I wondered if I could bother you again.
Man	Of course, what can I help you with?
Woman	Well, my flight home leaves tomorrow at 8am, and I wondered if it was best to take the train, bus or taxi?
Man	Hmmm. It's a tricky time, to be honest. The trains won't be running so early, but there's a shuttle bus that goes every hour on the hour – let me give you a leaflet.

4. You hear a station announcement about a delayed train. Passengers who want to go to Manchester should:

   A   wait for information.
   B   buy a new ticket.
   C   take another train.

Transcript

This is an announcement for all passengers on platform 6 who are waiting for the ten forty-seven train to Manchester. Unfortunately, this train is delayed by approximately 45 minutes. This is due to the fact that it is currently behind a broken-down train on the same track. We will provide updates as soon as we have more information. However, at the moment we advise all passengers wanting to go to Manchester to board the next train on platform 6 and change at Birmingham. If you need to change your ticket, please go to the information desk and they will exchange it for you for no charge.

5. You hear two friends talking about booking tickets. They agree to:

   A   wait until later.
   B   get them in person.
   C   sit separately.

Transcript

Woman	I keep refreshing the page, but I still can't find seats for us all together.
Man	Keep looking, though. I don't think we'll find anything better if we leave it any longer.
Woman	Do you think it might be better if we go down to the ticket office and ask?
Man	I don't think so. After all, surely their screens are showing the exact same thing as ours.
Woman	Hmmm. Maybe you're right.
Man	Look, I think we should just get what's available, even if we're in two different blocks. After all, we're there to hear the music!
Woman	Yes, you're right. I suppose there's no use waiting!

6. You hear a gardener talking about his work. What does he dislike about his job?

   A   The salary is quite low.
   B   The work is unpredictable.
   C   The schedule is exhausting.

Transcript

You know, I do feel extremely lucky because I get to spend my working days out in nature rather than sitting at a computer all day long – I can't imagine being stuck inside all day, to be honest. But don't get me wrong, there are some downsides as well. Sometimes we have to work long hours, especially in the spring when there's so much planting to be done, but the main issue is that it's seasonal work. I worry about the months when there's far less work, and it means I have to budget carefully throughout the year and make sure I save money for when work is more limited.

7. You hear two friends talking about online shopping. What annoys the man?

   A   Poor products
   B   Slow payment
   C   Delivery charges

Transcript

Woman	I picked up a great bargain online last night – a coffee table for only 50 pounds!
Man	Well, let's hope it's what you want.
Woman	What do you mean?

Man	Obviously it depends on the site, but I find lots of these things are not as good as they first appear.
Woman	Really?
Man	Yes. I bought some bedside tables that were basically full of scratches and dents – *and* it took about three weeks for them to arrive.
Woman	That's terrible, but I suppose I just find it far more convenient to shop online. Even dealing with a slow website is quicker than going to the shops.
Man	No doubt it's quicker, but you can sometimes pay for it in the end by choosing speed over quality.

8. You hear a teacher talking to her students. What is she telling them about?

A   Changes to exam dates.

B   Arrangements for a trip.

C   An important email.

Transcript

Okay everyone – sit down and pay attention. I need to give you some important information about the trip we're going on next week. Because it's after your final exams at the end of the month, we've decided you should get to choose where we go. Your parents will receive a message from the principal with all the options, and you'll need to reply with your first and second choices by Friday. Please remind your parents that they have to tick the box saying they agree. We need their permission, otherwise you won't be able to take part in the trip and I don't want that to happen to anyone.

Part 1: Put it to the test 2 | Answers   (pages 109–110)

1. You hear two people talking about an art exhibition. What do they agree about?

A   The artist was brilliant.

B   It needed more artworks.

C   The works were confusing.

Transcript

Woman	I can't believe the artist was at her own exhibition!
Man	Yes, it was brilliant! Great to get some idea of what was going through her head when she made the pieces.
Woman	Absolutely. Without that I would have been completely lost.

Man	You're not the only one! I think it's always a bit difficult to work out what is going on in an abstract piece.
Woman	Still, considering she's only been painting for seven years, she's done an impressive amount of paintings.
Man	Well, I thought there might have been some more to be honest, but I still really enjoyed what I saw. We should go to more things like this!

2. You hear two people talking about buying a new car. What is important for the woman?

   A   Brand
   B   Size
   C   Cost

Transcript

Woman	I've been having real difficulties trying to find a new car.
Man	Well, they're pretty expensive nowadays, even the second-hand ones.
Woman	Yes, but that's not really the issue. I'd be happy to spend quite a lot, but finding something suitable is proving to be tricky.
Man	But I thought you were happy with your car?
Woman	Well, it used to be fine but now that I've got a dog I feel like I need something with more boot space. However, many of the ones I've looked at don't look like they would fit much in.
Man	Hmmm. That's a shame. Perhaps you should ask around to see if anyone has any suggestions for good car companies.

3. You hear a tour guide talking about a city. Why does he recommend the old town?

   A   To hear traditional music.
   B   To eat cheaply.
   C   To see great architecture.

Transcript

If you've only got a few days in this city, make sure you go and see the old town. Well, we call it 'old' but actually a lot of it has been rebuilt over the years, so it isn't that great for fans of traditional architecture. However, the old town is absolutely THE place for seeing local people singing the tunes that have been the heart and soul of this city for hundreds of years. There are plenty of cafés and restaurants there, and they're very popular with tourists. Because of this, the prices aren't as reasonable as other areas in town, but the experience more than makes up for that.

4. You hear part of an interview with an actor. How did he get started in his career?

- A He met a director by chance.
- B He was hired by an agency.
- **C He applied for a lot of roles.**

Transcript

Woman	You've been in quite a few movies recently, but I'm sure people are keen to know how you got started.
Man	Okay. Well, my story is rather dull actually.
Woman	Oh, really? I thought perhaps you were spotted by a talent agent at acting school.
Man	No, nothing like that. For me it was just all hard work. After acting school, I spent three years trying to get acting job parts. It was quite depressing to get rejected a lot, but finally I got a small part in a movie that was a box office hit. I know lots of people have stories where they were working in a restaurant and served a director lunch one day, but not me.

5. You will hear a man leaving an answerphone message. What is the main reason for his message?

- A To promise something
- **B To blame someone**
- C To praise somewhere

Transcript

Hi there. It's John Sanders here, marketing director in head office. I'm just calling to talk about the work event we had last week at the Royston Centre. I'm not sure who booked it, but it was completely unsuitable for a company event. It's more like a community centre! That might be fine for some groups of people, but not for a world-leading manufacturer like us. Whoever it was who booked this needs to be spoken to, as far as I'm concerned. I mean, it's your department's job to get these kinds of things right. I'd also like you to guarantee that places are checked more carefully in the future. Thank you.

6. You hear two people talking about changes in their town. What does the woman think about the art gallery?

- **A It is a positive addition to the town.**
- B It will be welcomed by residents.
- C It has changed the look of the town.

B2 Listening | Part 1 | Answers

> **Transcript**

Woman	I visited the new art gallery in the town centre the other day, and **I was really impressed**. I mean, the design is not really to my taste but that's not the point. I think the gallery space works well and **it'll attract tourists too**.
Man	I'm not sure local people want even more tourists in the town centre, but I actually like the building. I think having something a bit more modern is a nice contrast to all the historical buildings there.
Woman	Well, I'm sure **it'll be popular with the younger generation**, especially the current exhibition all about the history of street art.

> Check your answer by trying to rule out the other two options. You will have a second chance to listen to the extracts and check your answer.

7. You hear two people talking about a trip. What are they discussing?

   A The transport
   B The accommodation
   C The day trips

> **Transcript**

Man	Hmmm. **I'm not sure we should stay in the middle of nowhere.**
Woman	Why not? The city will be full of tourists out on trips, and I'd rather avoid the crowds.
Man	Yes, I understand that, but we only have one car and there's eight of us. It'll be impossible for us all to get there as there'll be no public transport that reaches that far out.
Woman	Hmmm… I suppose you have a point there. It's disappointing though.
Man	Maybe we can find a compromise and **get somewhere in a village not too far away from the nearest bus, and we'd still be able to go on trips easily.**
Woman	Okay, **let's have a look on the web for more options**.

8. You hear a student talking about finishing her university course. How does she feel about the experience?

   A It made her more realistic.
   B It was too competitive.
   C It changed her work goals.

Transcript

I can't believe it's all over really. The course was very intense, and we all had to work extremely hard, but everyone was really supportive – it wasn't like some courses where the students are always trying to do better than each other. The assignments were tough, but they gave me real insight into the world of fashion design and I'm grateful for that. I think before, my understanding of the industry was too innocent, but at least now I know what to expect. Overall, I really enjoyed the course and I'd recommend it to anyone who is passionate about getting into fashion.

Part 2: Practise 1 | Answers (page 112)

Nick was originally interested in being a (1)_____.

> Noun – job: doctor, teacher, police officer?

While he was at university, Nick worked at a (2)_____.

> Noun – place: restaurant, clothes shop, supermarket

Nick's (3)_____ were pleased that he decided to be a chef.

> Noun – group of people (it must be plural because 'were' follows the space) – friends, parents, brothers, teachers

Doing a college course gave Nick some (4)_____ for cookery.

> Noun – (plural because of 'some'): ideas, money, experience, enjoyment

Part 2: Practise 2 | Answers (pages 112–113)

Nick was originally interested in being a (1) **lawyer**.

While he was at university, Nick worked at a (2) **bike shop**.

Nick's (3) **housemates** were pleased that he decided to be a chef.

Doing a college course gave Nick some (4) **(basic) skills** for cookery.

Transcript (Part 1)

Hello. My name is Nick, and I'm going to tell you all about what it takes to be a chef. Now, I didn't always want to be a chef but I was always interested in food. You see, my dad is a farmer and I grew up helping out a lot. But actually, I wanted to be a lawyer. It sounded much more exciting! (1)

It all changed when I went to university, though, and I started cooking my own food. I found that more interesting than my degree course. I used to study during the day and then get cooking books out of the library to find out more about it. I did all that while helping out at a bike shop, and I spent everything that I made there on trying new foods. (2)

I decided at the end of my degree that I wanted to be a chef. It was a bit of a shock for my parents, who thought I had wasted my time at university, but my housemates were really supportive of me. But they had tasted the food I'd learnt to cook, and they knew I had talent. (3)

So, I started looking for training courses. I could have done another degree, but I wanted practical experience in a kitchen. I ended up doing a part-time course and also working as an apprentice chef part-time too. I picked up lots of basic skills on the course, like working with meat and how to store foods, and I learnt creativity and speed in the restaurant. (4)

Don't write too much. Answers will be no more than three words in length.

Part 2: Practise 3 | Answers (page 113)

Nick thinks that the **(5)** _hours_ is the hardest thing about being a chef.

At first, Nick couldn't add much **(6)** _creativity_ to his dishes.

Nick thinks the best dish on the menu is the **(7)** _(whole) salmon_.

Nick tries to avoid making **(8)** _desserts_ if he can.

The approach of **(9)** _sharing (food)_ makes Nick's restaurant different from others.

Nick recommends gaining some **(10)** _experience_ as a first step into being a chef.

Transcript (Part 2)

A lot of people say that the most difficult thing about being a chef is the pressure. The kitchen is a busy place – but for me that's exciting. The hours, though, are probably the most challenging part. I often miss family gatherings and normally I don't finish until midnight. (5)

I'm used to it now, however. And I wouldn't swap my job for anything. It's ten years since I trained, and now I work as a head chef. It's a brilliant position as I get to show my creativity, which was much harder to do when I started out. Then, my dishes needed to be exactly how someone else told me to do them. (6)

We've got plenty of dishes on the menu, and most of them I've come up with myself. Our most popular dish by far is the rib of beef, but my personal favourite is the whole salmon. It's the most expensive dish we serve, but it's absolutely worth it! We serve lots of fish dishes, actually. I developed a love of fish cookery when I was doing my training, as well as pasta-making, which I find really relaxing. I do, however, try to stay out of one section of the kitchen where possible – desserts aren't for me! Every chef has their limits, and my talents just aren't in that area! But thankfully I have some very talented chefs who can do desserts far better than me! (7) (8)

We've always wanted to be inventive in the restaurant, and I think we've achieved that. So many restaurants in this city are similar. We wanted to stand out, so we decided to make our restaurant all about sharing food. So, our dishes will feed two or three people. It's a great way to eat. (9)

Cooking is a really creative job, and I'd recommend it to anyone. Of course, you must have a love of food, but most of all you need dedication. If you think it's the job for you, try to get some experience in a restaurant first of all. That will give you a taste of the job, and then you'll know if you'd like to work towards some qualifications. (10)

Part 2: Put it to the test 1 | Answers (page 114)

Grace thinks the best thing about the island is the **(1)**____peace____.

Visitors can often view different types of **(2)**__sea birds__ from the boat.

After some people going to **(3)**____Iceland____ stopped at the island, it became famous.

(4)__(Tour) boats__ are too large to get into the cave.

Its alternative name probably comes from a visit by a **(5)**____composer____.

B2 Listening | Part 2 | Answers

The **(6)** _(stormy) winters_ caused the only people living on the island to leave.

The only building on the island is a **(7)** _shelter_.

The island is now owned by a **(8)** _charity_.

You can walk up to the **(9)** _highest point_ during the tours.

It's a good idea to look at the **(10)** _weather forecast_ before going on a tour.

Transcript

We've got lots of tours to the island of Staffa, and it's quite a special place to see. We often ask our visitors what they enjoyed most about it, and they usually say the nature. But personally I love the island for its peace. There's no one around for miles, and it just makes you feel so relaxed. You'll see what I mean if you go there! **(1)**

The *only* way to reach the island is via boat. It takes about an hour, and if you're lucky you'll get a view of the dolphins which occasionally swim in these waters. You're sure to see lots of sea birds there, though, and there is quite a variety of these. The boats usually have binoculars so you can get a closer look. **(2)**

Little is known about the island's early history, but for a while it became quite a popular tourist destination. It became more well-known after a visit from Englishman Joseph Banks and Daniel Solander, from Sweden. They were scientists who stopped at the island on their way to Iceland. As they were so impressed by the island they wrote about it, starting its steady stream of visitors. **(3)**

They were impressed by the nature of the island, but particularly a cave in the cliffs. This is really what made the island stand out for them. The cave is a sea cave, but while it's possible for walkers to get through the small entrance on foot there is a natural path along the bottom of the cliffs – it's too small for the tour boats, so, if the weather is nice, the best way to enter is to swim in – or you can always hire kayaks. **(4)**

This cave is called Fingal's Cave, but it's also known to some people as the Musical Cave. This is probably because it inspired composer Felix Mendelssohn to write a piece of music after visiting it. It's also been the inspiration for painters and writers too. The cave is unlike others in the area as it's formed of columns. It looks like something a human might build, but it's completely natural. **(5)**

Nobody lives on the island these days, but there is a record of a single family living there hundreds of years ago. It was probably a difficult life for them, and in the end they left the island. You'd think living there would have been too lonely, but actually it was the stormy winters that made life there simply too difficult. The farmhouse they lived in isn't there anymore. In fact, the only place still standing is a shelter used by travellers. **(6)** **(7)**

There aren't even toilets there! But don't worry: there are facilities on the boats!

Staffa Island was owned by a private individual for a long time, and then in 1986 it was given to a charity that works on preserving the area. This is great for visitors because it means the island is protected as well as all its wildlife. (8)

You definitely won't regret going on a tour of the island. It isn't that big, and there's a walking trail that you can do which takes around half an hour. You can pretty easily get up to the highest point and then see great views of the surrounding islands. Most boats stop if they can, so you will have a chance to explore. (9)

And that's one thing I need to mention about the tours. If the sea is rough, then the boats can't land on the island. So, make sure to check the weather forecast. Normally the tour leaders will let you know if there is a problem, but it's a good idea to check before you book too. (10)

Part 2: Put it to the test 2 | Answers   (page 115)

The residents in Martin's block of flats wanted the garden to be used for (1) __relaxation__.

Adding some (2) __flowers__ will make the community garden brighter and more attractive.

The residents (3) __share__ the various jobs that need doing in the garden.

Martin was surprised that he needed a lot of (4) __time__ to do the spraying.

The covered (5) __seating area__ means that people can be in the garden all year round.

Martin noticed that the residents (6) __behave__ differently because of the garden.

Community gardens in cities highlight the importance of (7) __nature__ and connection.

It is common to see gardens on (8) __office blocks__ and public buildings.

Martin points out that the roofs of city buildings are often (9) __empty__.

The residents might invest in **(10)** _equipment_ so they can use rainwater in the garden.

Transcript

I live in a block of flats, and it has always had some grass all around it which no one really used. At a residents' meeting last year, we discussed what to do with it and there were various suggestions. But what most people said was they wanted a garden – not for growing vegetables or having barbecues, but as a quiet space for relaxation for all the residents. **(1)**

So, this spring we got started. We planted some bushes and some small fruit trees that grow quickly to give some shade for the summer. At the moment the garden is a bit dull, and we want to encourage more people to enjoy it all year round. This means we'll need to plant a lot more flowers and find out what will bring colour in different seasons. **(2)**

If people are interested in gardening, they can help grow the plants, but they don't have to. What we do ask is that residents volunteer for all the necessary tasks. Things like watering the plants, checking for insects, cutting back the trees and so on. We decided to share all the work rather than paying a gardener to do it. The garden is quite large, and the residents would prefer to spend their money on flowers and trees and equipment instead. It's a lot of work, though. We made a list of all the tasks to do over the year to help us get organised. I volunteered to spray the plants – I couldn't believe how much time it took! Next time I think I'll ask for some help! **(3)** **(4)**

So far, I think everyone is delighted with what we've done. On sunny days the whole neighbourhood is outside enjoying the space or working to improve it. But actually, even when the weather isn't so great residents use the garden. We built a seating area with a roof on top and some people even come out in the rain and snow! **(5)**

Another benefit that the garden has brought is that people are getting to know each other better. I've been observing how people behave in the garden, and everyone is much more chatty now. I found out that one of my neighbours was born in the same part of the country as me and another loves hiking like I do. We're arranging a trip together for next month! Benefits like these have made community gardens quite common in cities nowadays. The idea is to bring a little bit of the countryside into our urban spaces and make us feel healthier. These gardens brighten up city environments. They remind us that we should spend time in nature and increase communication with the people around us. **(6)** **(7)**

And, of course, they're good for the environment too. You might have seen a few on top of office blocks, as well as on other large buildings like museums, hospitals and libraries. All the extra plants improve the air quality in cities, and they provide habitats for birds and insects like bees. I don't understand why more buildings don't have them. **(8)**

There are so many empty roofs, and all that space could be used for community gardens. I mean, they're not being used for anything else, so it seems like such a waste. **(9)**

What I especially like about many rooftop gardens is the chance to collect rainwater rather than letting it disappear down the pipes. <mark>We are thinking of trying to do this in our garden, but not on the roof of the block of flats. There's a lot of equipment you can buy that collects rainwater on the ground.</mark> Our aim is to recycle it back into the garden so we don't have use water from the flats. We have lots of future plans for our garden! (10)

Part 3: Practise 1 | Answers   (page 118)

The question focuses on the main goal of practising sport.

A   to train with other people more

> **train** = play, practise / **other people** = other players, competitors

B   to increase their physical strength

> **increase** = improve, raise, get better / **physical strength** = muscles, body, strong, powerful

C   to become more sociable

> **more sociable** = friendly, go out more, attend events, meet more people

D   to strengthen their determination

> **strengthen** = improve, build up, increase / **determination** = motivation

E   to implement a routine

> **implement** = put in place, have, get, develop / **routine** = schedule, timetable, habits

F   to win a competition

> **win** = come first, be the best / **competition** = game, race, match, tournament

G   to improve a specific technique

> **improve** = increase, get better, develop / **specific technique** = method, approach, skill

H   to manage stress from work

> **manage** = cope with, face, deal with
> **stress** = stressful situations, problems
> **work** = in my job, at the office

Part 3: Practise 2 | Answers (pages 118–119)

A to train with other people more
B to increase their physical strength
C to become more sociable
D to strengthen their determination
E to implement a routine
F to win a competition
G to improve a specific technique
H to manage stress from work

Speaker 1: **1 B**
Speaker 2: **2 E**

Speaker 1

I'm training for a marathon next year. I don't think it will be too difficult because I've run some 10K races before. I'm quite self-motivated and have created my own schedule: I run three times a week before work and then once at the weekend with my running club. But the thing I'm a little bit concerned about is whether I'm strong enough. I'm going to need to spend a lot more time in the gym doing weights and exercises to build up my leg muscles. At the moment they're good for short distances, but I have to change this if I want to actually finish a marathon.

Speaker 2

I took up yoga last year because I work long hours at a computer and was suffering from hip pain. At first, I found it hard to build time for yoga into my daily life. I was always distracted by something. I decided to join a class, which gave me some structure, and the classes started to make a difference – and now I feel more motivated to do it at home. I aim to plan my home yoga sessions at the beginning of each week and make sure that nothing gets in the way. I've got quite a busy and stressful life, but I'm sure I can devote time to it.

Part 3: Practise 3 | Answers (page 119)

A	to train with other people more	Speaker 3:	**3 D**
B	to increase their physical strength	Speaker 4:	**4 C**
C	to become more sociable	Speaker 5:	**5 G**
D	to strengthen their determination		
E	to implement a routine		
F	to win a competition		
G	to improve a specific technique		
H	to manage stress from work		

Speaker 3

I'm quite a sporty person, so when one of my work colleagues suggested we play golf together I thought it was a great idea. The only problem is that I'm a terrible golfer, even after having had lessons for a few months. But I'm not going to give up like I did with tennis last year. I know it'll take time to improve, and I just have to work at it. My golf coach used to be a professional player, and she says I just have to stay positive whenever I make mistakes. I love the community spirit of the place, though. There's a great atmosphere, and I've met so many nice people at the different events they have.

Speaker 4

Recently, I noticed that I haven't been as involved in my badminton club as lots of the other members. I usually just chat with a couple of friends who I play games with. Anyway, I've decided to attend the club dinners that are held at the end of each month after the club competitions. I'd like to get know everyone more, even if I am a bit shy. I think it'd be good for my game too – you know, talking about techniques and different types of shots. I don't really know which aspects of my game I should work on, so it might have an extra benefit if I learn something too.

Speaker 5

My swimming club is a really social place. I love taking part in the competitions that they organise. I've been improving my strength a lot recently by training more regularly. I also got a coach to identify areas for improvement. My diving is the issue, though, and I should try not to splash as much. My coach has videoed me so that he can explain what I'm doing wrong. I didn't think I was that motivated to improve, but the more I train the more this is starting to change. I'm becoming more competitive as I get better.

Part 3: Put it to the test 1 | Answers   (page 120)

A	Thinks it's too complicated	Speaker 1:	**1** E
B	Enjoys the sense of adventure	Speaker 2:	**2** F
C	Makes them feel nervous	Speaker 3:	**3** A
D	Prefers flying alone	Speaker 4:	**4** H
E	Finds it uncomfortable	Speaker 5:	**5** D
F	Likes the service		
G	Enjoys the luxury		
H	Likes looking out the window		

Speaker 1

I never particularly enjoyed flying when I was younger. I was a bit afraid of it, to be honest, but now I don't mind it at all. I mean, it's a quick way to travel. Of course, at one metre ninety tall, the seats aren't perfect for me, and I suppose that's my major problem with it, but I try to get up and move about the cabin as much as I can, and I never choose a window seat as I think they're the worst for someone like me! When I'm travelling for work, though, they fly me business class, which is much better – in all areas.

Speaker 2

I'm used to flying. My parents always took me on overseas holidays, and now I fly almost every week for work. It's never much of an adventure, though, as I always go back and forth to the same place: London to New York! I get quite bored sometimes, just staring out at the same old view of the Atlantic, but I've got to say the cabin staff are excellent, and nothing is too much trouble for them. Although, I think they probably know me by now, as I always fly from the same airports and on the same airline! Of course, I'd prefer to fly less, especially because of the environment, but I need to do it for my job.

Speaker 3

The thought of flying away to some amazing destination on holiday is always exciting, but I don't think the reality is quite the same. Normally, the travelling part of the holiday is far from a luxury. The size of the airports, having to go through security checks, endless queueing to get on the plane and trying to find your gate in time – it gets on my nerves! I miss those simple days of just getting in the car and heading to the coast. That's what I used to do with my parents. And we'd look out onto the countryside, singing songs. Those were the days!

Speaker 4

I don't understand people who worry about flying. After all, it's one of the safest forms of travel. I certainly find it an enjoyable way to get from A to B. It used to be a real experience, with great service and everything. I don't think it's quite the same these days, but there's nothing better than watching the clouds pass you by or spotting a mountain or city far below. I suppose, when I think of it, it's my favourite way to travel. I kind of feel like the airplane is my safe place. I'm often more worried about what's going to happen at the other end, like if I can't get to my hotel from the airport or something. Then, the adventure really begins!

Speaker 5

I suppose I don't mind flying, but I don't particularly enjoy it either. You see, I get quite easily bored on a plane, especially on a longer flight. After all, there's not particularly anywhere to go or anything to do. Add onto that the time it takes to get through security and passport control, and it can seem like forever. Although, I must say, it's much worse when I fly with others, especially the kids. It's far more stressful for me even though they think it's a great adventure! Once they made so much noise, I felt completely uncomfortable for the whole flight.

Part 3: Put it to the test 2 | Answers   (page 120)

A   The worry of being a new student   Speaker 1: | 1 | F |
B   The assistance from the staff   Speaker 2: | 2 | H |
C   The design of the building   Speaker 3: | 3 | B |
D   The excitement of making friends   Speaker 4: | 4 | D |
E   The personality of their teacher   Speaker 5: | 5 | G |
F   The equipment in their classroom
G   The number of people
H   The range of fun activities

Speaker 1

I think it was enjoyable overall due to the amount of new and interesting experiences we had on that day. I made some new friends, I met a lot of adults who weren't like my parents and I got to play in an enormous playground. But I think what particularly stood out was seeing everything there was to help us learn. The teacher showed us the cupboards where all the pens and paints and books and calculators were kept. It was like being in a cave full of treasure! To be honest, a lot of my other memories have faded and I wish I was able to remember more about my teacher and my classmates.

Speaker 2

The school I went to as a child was completely new, so everyone in the area was really excited about seeing it for the first time. The facilities were modern, and there was a computer room too. It had that smell that all new buildings have. We did so many things – games, painting, singing and running around in the playground – and I thought it was all amazing. A few of the other children in my class started crying when their parents left, but not me! I don't really remember much about my teacher on that day. Probably because there were so many different teachers and we met lots of other staff members too.

Speaker 3

My parents were quite nervous about me starting school because I was shy when I was younger. But they shouldn't have worried at all because the staff were always checking if the students were okay. I can clearly remember that I got lost on my way to the toilet because the building was so enormous. Anyway, one of the cleaning staff found me and showed me where to go, which I was really relieved about. I told my parents about it, which I think made them more relaxed because they saw that it wasn't just the teachers who were kind and that everyone there wanted to look after us.

Speaker 4

In the weeks leading up to the beginning of term, I kept asking my parents so many questions about school. Would my teacher be friendly, how many kids would be in my class, how big was the school, and so on. As an only child, the idea of school was really appealing to me. I couldn't wait to meet my classmates and find out what they were like. And I was not disappointed! The other children were super friendly, and we all got on well together – well, most of the time. Except when we thought someone had taken our calculator or tablet or something like that.

Speaker 5

The staff were probably exhausted by the end of that first day since quite a lot of children seemed to be nervous and wouldn't let go of their parents. I'd never seen that many children in one building before! Everywhere you looked, children were running around, shouting and screaming with either excitement or fear. Although I'll never forget it, I wasn't concerned about it though – coming from a large family, I'm used to noise. I don't recall much about the classroom activities, but we might have played some games. You know, I'm still friends with a couple of people I met on that first day all these years later.

Part 4: Practise 1 | Answers (page 122)

1. Alex believes summer camps are a <u>good experience</u> because:
2. How are summer camps <u>different from school</u>?
3. What does Alex say <u>teenagers develop</u> on the camp?

A	Things that teenagers learn on summer camps	✓
B	A description of different types of summer camp	☐
C	Why teenagers prefer summer camps to school	☐
D	How to help teenagers who get homesick	☐
E	A comparison with school activities	✓
F	Advantages of attending a summer camp	✓

Part 4: Practise 2 | Answers (pages 122–123)

1. Alex believes summer camps are a good experience because:

   A they only last a short time.
   B the staff are well qualified.
   C there is a range of activities on offer.

2. How are summer camps different from school?

   A They have more activities.
   B They are more flexible.
   C They focus more on skills.

3. What does Alex say teenagers develop on the camp?

   A Leadership skills
   B Independence
   C Self confidence

Extract 1

Interviewer   I'm joined this morning by Alex Blakely, manager of the UK's largest summer camp. He believes that all parents should seriously consider sending their teenagers on a summer camp. So, tell us Alex, why are you convinced that this is such as great idea?

Alex	Hello. Well, for me it's about opening their eyes to new things. In their daily lives, teenagers might go to a dance class or play a sport or attend a weekly group like Scouts. But here they're able to try out so many things they've never done before. Our staff have a lot of experience working with young people, and we really want them to make the most of their time with us. After all, most participants only spend two or three weeks at camp.
Interviewer	Some parents don't want to pay for an experience that they feel is similar to school. What is your opinion on this?
Alex	Even though the teenagers are a similar age, and the activities are all learning experiences, summer camps are unique. This is because there is a lot more freedom. We don't have a prescribed programme. Also, we encourage participants to get involved with as many or as few activities as they want.
Interviewer	What skills do teenagers learn at the camp?
Alex	At this age, young people are developing their identity quite rapidly. We're keen to show them ways to do this successfully. Although they cannot be fully in charge of their day-to-day lives, we want them to grow as people. Positive learning experiences at the camp make students see their abilities more clearly.

1 C
2 B
3 C

Part 4: Practise 3 | Answers (pages 123–124)

4. What do the camp counsellors help teenagers do?

   A solve friendship issues.
   B be more emotional.
   C learn how to argue.

5. Why are teenagers not allowed mobile phones at the camp?

   A to help them rely on technology less.
   B to prevent contact with their parents.
   C to improve communication skills.

6. When choosing a summer camp, parents prefer places that:

   A are convenient to get to.
   B offer water sports.
   C other parents recommend.

Watch out for **distractors** – information that may lead to choosing a wrong answer!

7. After summer camp, parents often report that their children:

  A keep the house tidier.

  B get up earlier in the morning.

  C organise themselves better.

Extract 2

Interviewer What about teenagers who are nervous about attending a summer camp?

Man Some parents worry about this. Remember that the staff are trained in techniques for communicating with young people. Everyone has a personal counsellor who helps smooth over any disagreements. We resolve all conflicts as they happen to show how to build relationships but also how to manage conflict. Part of the experience we offer is the opportunity to communicate with adults who are not parents or teachers. **4 | A**

Interviewer Do you allow the use of mobile phones on the camp?

Man That's an excellent question and one we get asked all the time. We state very clearly that teenagers have to leave their mobile phones at home. This is not because we don't want them using technology – we have tablets and laptops for our creative activities. The reason is that we don't want them calling home all the time because parents tend to worry. Also, they've come to the camp to make friends and have fun outside, not spend all day on social media. **5 | B**

Interviewer Talking of nature, how important is the location of summer camps in general?

Man Most of them are chosen because they are near rivers or lakes so that water sports can be included on the programme. This is one of the biggest attractions for most camps. But parents are usually thinking about the drive! If they're too remote, or the journey is complicated, parents are likely to think twice because of the inconvenience. So that is always considered when choosing venues. **6 | A**

Interviewer And finally, in your experience, what changes do parents notice most when their children return from camp?

Man Um, I think what they see immediately is how their children have become better able to care for themselves in general. Camp teaches them to get themselves together in the mornings. We expect them to be on time for activities and bring everything they need. Some parents also say their children are more willing to help around the house, perhaps helping with dinner or cleaning the car. **7 | C**

Interviewer These are all good benefits! Okay, well that's all we have time for. Thank you, Alex.

Part 4: Put it to the test 1 | Answers (pages 124–125)

1. What does Victoria say about studying to be a vet?

   A It was harder than she expected.

   B She adapted to the course demands.

   C It was a rewarding experience.

2. According to Victoria, team meetings help the vets:

   A deal with stressful situations.

   B make decisions more quickly.

   C come up with new approaches.

3. Why is talking to pet owners difficult for vets?

   A They are very emotional.

   B They can be unpredictable.

   C They want positive news.

4. Working as a farm vet helped Victoria to:

   A rely on her knowledge.

   B improve her communication.

   C manage her schedule.

5. What did Victoria admire about farmers?

   A Their approach to animals' health issues.

   B The way they communicate with vets.

   C How they care for their animals.

6. Victoria thinks that managing a veterinary practice:

   A is something she would like to do one day.

   B could become boring after a while.

   C would not be the best use of her skills.

7. How has technology affected Victoria's job?

   A The paperwork has been reduced.

   B The practice has more customers.

   C The staff have become more efficient.

Extract 1

Interviewer   Working as a vet is a childhood dream for many people. However, it takes many years of study and hard work. Today, I'm speaking to Victoria Bradshaw about the challenges and rewards of this demanding job. Firstly, Victoria, did you enjoying studying veterinary science at university?

Woman   I must admit that at times I wondered if I'd done the right thing. The course is long and there is so much to learn. However, after my first year I noticed that it became easier. Or perhaps I just got tougher and more able to deal with the workload. I'm glad I stuck it out because I really enjoy my job. Every day I get to feel good, so it's very rewarding.   **1 | B**

Interviewer   Can you tell us a little bit about your day-to-day work?

Woman   Of course. We start at about 8.00 am with a team meeting to review all the animals that are being treated. Getting together means that we can benefit from talking through different treatments. Often this leads to fresh ideas about what to do or why a different medicine might work better. These meetings are vital for building confidence and sharing ideas.   **2 | C**

Interviewer   What other skills do you need besides medical skills?

Woman   We need to be able to communicate well. Most of the animals we see are pets, so there's a lot of talking to owners. Vets new to the job often find this upsetting. You never really know how someone is going to react to news, even when it's positive. But you have to get used to it and find a way to deal with it if you want to work as a vet.   **3 | B**

Interviewer   Have you always worked with pets?

Woman   Actually, I started out as a farm vet. The structure of that job is very different. You spend most of the time out and about on farm visits. And you spend a lot of time alone and don't have the chance to discuss things with your colleagues. But for me it was an excellent way to become more confident in my abilities. I had to get on with it and trust my instincts.   **4 | A**

Interviewer   Did you enjoy working with farm animals and farmers?

Woman   Yes, I did. During my training I became interested in the challenges of treating large animals. But soon I realised that a large part of the job is talking to farmers. You have to work hard to earn their trust because they already know so much about caring for and treating their own animals. I think this was why it was hard for me to communicate with pet owners at first. Because I'd spent so long with farmers who are much more practical about sickness and disease, I wasn't used to the emotional element required to work as a city vet.   **5 | A**

Interviewer   Yes, I see. Would you like to have your own veterinary practice one day?

Woman   It's something I have thought about, but I think my skills are more suited to animal care rather than people-management. I'm good at paperwork and keeping accurate records, but I'm less interested in hiring and training staff. And, of course, getting the right staff and keeping a team together is one of the most important parts of running a veterinary practice.   **6 | C**

Interviewer   And has your job changed much in recent years?

Woman   I think for me it's the amount we use technology, but not just for our medical work. Video calls, emails with photos and messaging on mobile phones means that we now provide services to more people, not just those who live nearby. It's transformed the practice and how we work compared to a decade ago…

| 7 | B |

Part 4: Put it to the test 2 | Answers   (pages 125–126)

1. Tom started playing chess because:

   A   he liked intellectual games.

   B   he wanted to please his parents.

   C   he had friends in a local club.

2. The thing that most interests Tom about chess is that:

   A   it involves a lot of luck.

   B   there are many strategies.

   C   each game is unique.

3. What do chess players begin to understand as they improve their skills?

   A   That it is more difficult than it appears

   B   That the rules are complicated

   C   That losing is good for learning

4. What are the benefits of playing chess for the brain?

   A   Improved intelligence

   B   Better overall function

   C   More creative thinking

5. What does Tom say about chess books?

   A   They help beginners get started.

   B   They are not worth the money.

   C   They are useful for advanced players.

6. Tom thinks that chess remains popular because:

   A   people of different ages like playing it.

   B   there are so many opportunities to play it.

   C   it is part of many cultures around the world.

7. What is Tom's assessment of playing chess against a computer?

    A It prepares players for competitions.

    B It provides limited practice.

    C It gives a wide range of practice.

Extract 1

Interviewer	With me today is Tom Lawrence, who has recently written a book called *The Excitement of Chess*. Tom, you've been playing chess as a hobby and in national competitions for many years. What got you into it?
Man	When I was a teenager, my parents were worried that I didn't have any non-academic interests. They kept trying to get me interested in sport or music. For me, though, strategy games that involve puzzles and working things out were more exciting than physical ones. One day, when I was looking around a second-hand shop, I saw a chess board and decided to buy it. I started to play with my best friend, and we both loved it. We joined a local club and I've never looked back.
Interviewer	That's a great story. Now, I'm sure not all our listeners would say that it's an exciting game so why do you think it is?
Man	I suppose it's the fact that every game is totally different. Even though players are using the same strategies and techniques, no two games are the same. I'm really intrigued by that idea, and I get a little rush of excitement every time the first piece is played in a game. Although, of course, like all strategy games, there is an element of luck too, which adds to the fun.
Interviewer	Does it take a long time to become a good player?
Man	You know, one of the beauties of the game is that it never gets boring. Although it is easy to learn, they say it takes a lifetime to master chess. This is probably due to the fact that the more you play and lose, the more you want to improve. As you get more involved and learn new tricks, you start to see how complex it can really be.
Interviewer	And what about people who are thinking of getting into chess for the intellectual factor? What would you say to them?
Man	Oh, I'd definitely encourage them to take up chess for that reason. There is overwhelming evidence that playing chess is good for the brain. Apparently, you use both sides of the brain when you play, which boosts your brain activity in all sorts of ways. Studies have shown that chess players remember more, their minds are sharper and they can focus better. I don't know if that makes them more intelligent though!
Interviewer	Would you recommend that people have lessons or just give it a go?
Man	Well, first of all, let me say that there are no barriers to entry in chess. Buying a board is cheap, and you don't need any expensive equipment or lessons to begin playing. Most people just practise and learn new tactics and strategies that way. I mean, there are thousands of books you could

1 A

2 C

3 A

4 B

B2 Listening | Part 4 | Answers

	buy to study the game, but it's not necessary. Perhaps, if you really get into it, you might consider buying a book to learn some of the classic moves by the grand masters.	5 C
Interviewer	Ah. Okay. And why do you think chess is still so popular?	
Man	Well, it's been around for so long, which means it's spread all over the world. And now it can be played online as well, which means it's a game that can bring people together in the virtual world as well as the real world.	6 B
Interviewer	And finally, what are your thoughts on playing chess against a computer?	
Man	Hmm. That's an interesting question! I would recommend it because all practice is good, but there are a couple of things to bear in mind. One is that computers are always logical when they play whereas humans are less predictable. I think you should practise with unexpected situations, too, and not just against computers, especially if you want to play in competitions.	7 B

Answers

Practice test 1 (pages 129–136)

Part 1

1 A 2 C 3 A 4 B 5 B 6 B 7 B 8 A

Part 2

9 (weight of) traffic
10 narrow
11 1970s / nineteen-seventies
12 retired people
13 steel
14 land
15 special days
16 birds
17 (desert) conditions
18 boat ride

Part 3

19 E 20 H 21 B 22 G 23 F

Part 4

24 C 25 B 26 C 27 C 28 A 29 B 30 A

Practice test 2 (pages 137–144)

Part 1

1 B 2 A 3 A 4 C 5 B 6 A 7 A 8 C

B2 Reading | Practice test | Answers

Part 2

9	pedestrians	14	human error
10	surveys	15	planting trees
11	crossing	16	distracting
12	eye contact	17	Driver Attention Monitor / DAM
13	Bright clothing	18	safety industry

Part 3

19 G   20 H   21 C   22 E   23 A

Part 4

24 C   25 C   26 A   27 B   28 A   29 B   30 C

Practice test 3 (pages 145–152)

Part 1

1 B   2 C   3 A   4 B   5 A   6 C   7 A   8 C

Part 2

9	achievement	14	cycle
10	everyday life	15	social media
11	art department	16	languages
12	audience	17	errors
13	budget	18	well-paid / well paid

Part 3

| 19 | D | 20 | B | 21 | A | 22 | G | 23 | F |

Part 4

| 24 | B | 25 | C | 26 | A | 27 | B | 28 | C | 29 | C | 30 | A |

Practice test 4 (pages 153–160)

Part 1

| 1 | C | 2 | A | 3 | B | 4 | A | 5 | C | 6 | C | 7 | A | 8 | B |

Part 2

9	(quite) keen	14	window cleaners
10	meeting point	15	lack of room
11	helicopter	16	(marked) paths
12	(changes in the) weather	17	hot chocolate
13	safety talk	18	mystery

Part 3

| 19 | C | 20 | F | 21 | E | 22 | B | 23 | H |

Part 4

| 24 | C | 25 | A | 26 | C | 27 | B | 28 | A | 29 | A | 30 | B |

Practice test 1: Transcript | Part 1 (pages 130–131)

Extract 1

Man Your daughter is making really good progress this year so far, and I'm really pleased.

Woman That is good news. I was worried that you were going to tell me something negative like she's always distracting the others or something.

Man Oh no! Overall, she's great to teach and I'm impressed with her ability to get on well with the other students in her class. She's quite confident and enjoys helping her classmates on projects. However, she could pay attention a bit more when I explain what we're doing. Sometimes, she makes mistakes and I think it's because of that.

Woman Okay. Well, we'll discuss this at home with her and see what we can do.

Extract 2

Woman You know, I'd definitely recommend that hotel to anyone traveling on business.

Man Absolutely. I mean, I know that the restaurant wasn't open when we arrived, but we knew it wouldn't be. I just couldn't believe that the receptionist had a list of all the local places printed out and ready for us!

Woman And remember when I couldn't print out my presentation for the meeting and someone drove to a printing shop for me?

Man Yes! I know it wasn't very far away, but they didn't have to do it. In a lot of hotels these days service isn't very good because the staff aren't allowed to make their own decisions on the spot like that.

Extract 3

I love growing tomatoes because their flavour is so much better than those you buy in the supermarkets. The key to growing successful tomatoes is to monitor them because they need a lot of water and sun. If your plants don't seem to be developing and getting stronger, you might need to move them. I plant several varieties of seeds in different parts of the garden in springtime and also some in plant pots because the soil in my garden isn't great. Every morning and evening during the growing season I check for insects and see which plants are dry. It's important to look for other clues like brown leaves too.

Extract 4

We have to increase renewable energy in this part of the country. But in my mind wind farms aren't as efficient as other sources such as solar. If the government gave us all some money to install solar panels on our roofs, it would be great. I mean, they don't take up as much space as wind farms. Also, I know plenty of people who would prefer wind farms not to be built in residential areas – they're always complaining about that. I wonder if they would be happier with solar instead? Especially if the local government helped out with the costs.

Extract 5

Woman	How can I help you today, sir?
Man	I'm looking for something smart to wear to a business event, but I don't want something too formal so perhaps a light colour?
Woman	What about this jacket over here? The style is very popular these days, especially with young executives aiming to give a good impression without coming across as too formal.
Man	It's very stylish, but I'm not sure I can afford it at the moment. It's just outside my price range, even though I'd love to have something like that in my wardrobe.
Woman	Okay, well we do have some similar styles I can show you which might be more affordable. Come over here…

Extract 6

The mayor's office has announced that the proposal for a new shopping centre has been approved. There was a lot of discussion about the location, and the initial suggestion of the site behind the train station was rejected. This was because the site is actually quite small. The construction company said that they wanted to provide plenty of parking. So, they finally persuaded the mayor's office that the best place for that was on the outskirts of the town. Even though it's a little further for customers to travel, businesses say that they are happy with the decision. They are going to build a children's playground as well as lots of parking.

Extract 7

Woman	You know, I wasn't sure if I would enjoy all these exercise classes when I joined the gym.
Man	I know what you mean. I thought they were pretty hard when I started, but they are definitely helping me get fit and I've noticed that I'm able to run more quickly than before.
Woman	That's great. I've been lifting some weights as well as doing the classes. I really believe that it'll help develop my muscles. I've already lost quite a lot of weight, but I still feel weak and so that's what I'm focusing on now.
Man	Well, I hope you start noticing a difference soon.
Woman	Me too!

> Be prepared to hear some or all the options, either directly or indirectly.

Extract 8

Woman Since I joined a few months ago, I can't believe how many interesting local people I've got to know.

Man Yeah, so have I – although I wasn't expecting that. My motivation was driven by the fact that I'd realised that I needed to discover new authors and not just read the same thing all the time.

Woman I decided to sign up for it so that I'd have more opportunities to talk about the things I was reading. My family don't really like talking about books very much, so I wanted to find some people like me.

Man Well, it sounds like it was a great decision for both of us.

Practice test 1: Transcript | Part 2 (page 132)

Extract

Welcome to Lake Havasu City, Arizona! Today, I'm going to tell you about our famous bridge, London Bridge. Now, I know what you're thinking – London Bridge? Shouldn't that be in England, not Arizona? Well, it used to be in London, but American businessman, Robert P. McCulloch, bought the bridge and moved it all the way here! It might seem strange to sell a bridge, but unlike many people had thought, the English didn't do it for money. It simply couldn't carry the weight of traffic on it anymore, so they had to replace it, and… get rid of the old one!

Now, this isn't actually the very first London Bridge. It has been rebuilt several times over hundreds of years. In fact, the bridge before this one had shops and houses on it. It seems dangerous, doesn't it? In fact, the problem was that it was narrow – there wasn't the space for many larger forms of transport to cross it, and so they built a larger bridge. This was in the 1830s. After 130 years of use in London, it was bought by McCulloch in the 1960s and it was officially opened in Arizona in the 1970s. At that time, Lake Havasu City was incredibly small. It had around 20 properties and just a handful of local people. This was largely because it was desert, and miles away from the major cities. But McCulloch had big plans. He was a housing developer and wanted to make the area popular, both with tourists, but also with retired people who he wanted to encourage to move there. His plan worked. Now, more than 50,000 people live in the city, and more than a million visitors come to see the bridge every year. That's a great number!

Interestingly, when they rebuilt the bridge here, they didn't rebuild it exactly. The internal structure, built originally in stone, was replaced with steel. This meant the bridge could be lighter but also stronger – but the stonework on the outside is all original. Also, the decision on where to build the bridge is quite interesting. Obviously, in London, the bridge crossed the famous Thames River, but here it wasn't built over a river but on land between the city centre and Pittsburgh Point. Some time after its building they redirected a canal through it, making Pittsburgh Point an island!

Now, let's take a look at the bridge… It's obviously a grey colour, but it's actually green too! This is because of the yellow LED streetlamps, which while keeping the traditional look use much less electricity than the old ones. We also celebrate special days by lighting the bridge up! For example, this evening it will be purple to celebrate a special football event in the city. I should also mention life on the bridge – obviously, no people live on it but plenty of other things do. People often see bats around the bridge, but the most common animals we see are birds. This is really great for the city, because, as you can imagine, in a desert there aren't many places for such animals to go. We also had a wild cat living inside the bridge for a few months too!

For many years now, this bridge has been the pride of the city. And we hope it will be with us for many hundreds of years to come. With the desert conditions, where there isn't much humidity or cold, the bridge requires little maintenance, and so it should last for years!

So, that's the end of the tour. There's plenty to do in town, if you'd like to have a look around. And if you'd like to go on a boat ride, you can get tickets in the visitor centre, which is right next to the bridge. They're only $2 and it's well worth it in my opinion.

Practice test 1: Transcript | Part 3 (page 133)

Extract 1

I moved to this village about two years ago and thought there would be a great sense of community in a smaller place, but actually, things were better in the city! Most of the time here, I don't even see another person in the street! It's so quiet. I suppose, when I go to the bakers or the post office, the staff in there always have time for a chat, and that hardly ever happened where I used to live. Also, I don't spend as much money as I used to either. That's probably a good thing. Perhaps I'm just not ready for the slower pace of life. I will hopefully get used to it in time.

Extract 2

Oh, I'm definitely glad I made the move to the countryside. It feels much healthier than being in the city, and, well, there's just more space to live. It does take me longer to get to work, though. It's about an hour on the train, but it's very reliable and I don't mind much because I just spend that time watching movies on my phone. Although the travel takes longer, I'd recommend living in the countryside to anyone, as long as they enjoy peace and quiet like me. It's perhaps not a life for people who like lots of excitement, but I find my life has improved in so many ways.

Extract 3

Moving to the countryside really opened my eyes to a different way of living. When I lived in the city, I was always out and about with my friends going to the cinema or restaurants, but we don't have any of those services here in the village. Instead, I spend a lot of time with my neighbours. We share the food we grow in our gardens and make sure we check up on the elderly people who live alone. I love being part of this, and now I wish I'd made more of an effort to be friendly when I lived in the city.

Extract 4

As much as I'm delighted to be living here because it's quiet and my neighbours are all really friendly, the village would benefit from having a bus service, or maybe a couple of shops or a café. We have to drive to the nearby town if we want to do any shopping. It's not very far, so it doesn't take long, but in my view more people would come to live here if we had a bit more to offer. Anyway, I'm happy overall because I was really fed up with the city. My commute was over an hour and travelling by train had become so expensive.

Extract 5

I left the city a few years ago and opened a bakery in a village in the countryside. Living here was quite a shock at the beginning, because I missed going to the theatre and seeing my friends who all still lived in the city, but I soon got used to it. I think the thing that has changed most for me is that I don't spend nearly as much as I used to. I mean, there are very few shops near me, so I do different things and I grow a lot of my own food now which means I go the supermarket less.

Practice test 1: Transcript | Part 4 (pages 134–135)

Extract

Man	Welcome to 'The Natural Beauty Show', Emily. Could you tell us more about why you started making your own skincare products?
Woman	Sure. And thanks for having me. I have a degree in biology, so I know quite a lot about plants and which ones are good for the skin. When my son was younger, he suffered from spots on his face and neck. Being a teenager, he was very embarrassed, and I thought I should try to do something about it. We'd tried lots of products before, but they were extremely expensive. So, I thought: why not try making something myself? They were successful for my son and soon his friends wanted some. Soon after that, I set up the business.
Man	What challenges did you experience when you started the business?
Woman	I know many small businesses say marketing is tricky, but this was okay for me because my son and his friends had already spread the word about my products. I'd had great feedback from all these teenagers, and everyone wanted more. That was the problem – I was so busy making skincare products that I didn't have time to

	explore other ideas. I wanted to read more about different plants, but I just couldn't.
Man	Hmm, did you manage to find a solution to this problem?
Woman	Well, lots of different people gave me advice, and my manager from my old job told me that I had to employ someone to make the products so that I could free up some time for the other parts of the business. I joined a club for small businesses in my area, and through them I found my first employee! I much prefer chatting with other businesspeople in this group to using online groups. It's more personal.
Man	Can you tell us about your typical day?
Woman	I start the day by replying to customers who aren't happy with our products. It isn't a nice job, so I always get it out of the way first. Then I can do something much more fulfilling – working on the text for the skincare products' packaging. People don't realise how much of a difference it makes. Oh, and of course, we have to comply with regulations for legal purposes. At the end of the day, we have a staff meeting to chat about how things are going and spend some time together.
Man	Do you have any recommendations for people who are thinking of starting a small business?
Woman	Hmm. There's so much information online these days, which is a great help. As far as I'm concerned, though, it's essential to find someone who you trust to do your finances. And someone professional as well. Friends and family can be good sources of recommendation in this area because lots of people need to use an accountant for personal things as well as business.
Man	Why do you think your products have become so popular?
Woman	I think it mostly comes down to the fact that I'm a biologist. Customers trust my knowledge and know that the ingredients in the products are used because there is evidence that they work. I mean, there are cheaper skincare ranges for skin problems – but some of them contain chemicals that might cause other issues, even if they do clear up spots.
Man	Finally, Emily. What is your view on the future of natural skincare products?
Woman	That's a good question! A current trend is adding a lot of vitamins and minerals to creams, but this probably won't last long. The focus is more likely to be on increasing the amount of packaging made from biodegradable materials. I mean, most companies are moving towards doing this now. There will probably be more and more interest in using organic ingredients, but this is less appealing to customers compared to packaging.
Man	Thank you, Emily. And that's all we have time for today…

Practice test 2: Transcript | Part 1 (pages 138–139)

Extract 1

Man   So, what did you think of it?

Woman   It was okay, but there were far too many people attending.

Man   Did you think?

Woman   Yes, it felt like some kind of conference session rather than a paid course. Fifty people is too many!

Man   I suppose that's true, but I still thought it was very useful. I think it's essential to learn presentation skills like that, and we've got lots to take home.

Woman   Yes, that's true. I think it was good overall. I just think in the feedback I'll mention that I think thirty should be the maximum size.

Extract 2

When the match ends, please remember that there are only three main exits: the East Exit, the Central Exit and the Durham Exit. The West Exit, which is normally for families to leave the stadium, is closed today due to building work outside the gate. We advise anyone with children to remain in their seats until the majority of spectators have left the stadium. If you are unsure of how to exit, staff will be in the stadium and will be happy to help. Please make sure you take all your rubbish with you when you leave the stadium and please do not run.

Extract 3

Woman   Excuse me. I'd like to take this phone back please. It's not working properly.

Man   I'm sorry about that. What's wrong with it exactly?

Woman   Well, I kept thinking the screen has turned off, but it seems that the phone has actually switched itself off.

Man   Hmmm. Do you think it's getting too hot?

Woman   It doesn't feel too hot. I think it's just not powering up properly.

Man   We'll check it out. Would you like a refund for it or a replacement?

Woman   Can I replace it with a different phone? I saw a cool phone near the entrance that looks great.

Man   Yes, of course.

If you find one question very hard, move on and come back to it later.

Extract 4

Man	I can't believe we're back at work tomorrow!
Woman	Yes, the holiday has ended too soon! But wasn't it nice?
Man	Yes, and the food was much better than I expected. In fact, I think I've put on weight!
Woman	Ha ha! Well, that often happens on holidays! If only we'd stayed in a different hotel, though.
Man	I know what you mean. It just needed a bit of decoration, didn't it? And some entertainment! But I'd definitely go back to the same resort. It had something for everyone.
Woman	Yes, even though we spent most of the days in the rain, it didn't seem to matter.
Man	Oh, it wasn't so bad. There were only a few days of bad weather.

Extract 5

I recently went to see 'Dust Bowl Mountain' at the cinema, and it was a pleasant surprise for me. It wasn't the usual kind of action film – it had a lot of emotion to it. The film was actually based on a book, but I don't necessarily think that means a film will be good. However, one of my fellow film buffs suggested that I see it, so I went in open-minded. He told me the director had done an excellent job with the film, and now I agree. I think I'll look out for more of his films in the future.

Extract 6

I suppose, when I went into the police force I thought it would be similar to what it's like when you see police on the TV. But I was surprised. I actually spend most of my days just walking around the streets talking to people. It's actually a lot less scary than I thought it might be. And there are lots of different jobs to do in the day. In fact, you've got to have writing skills and computer skills, so it's not perhaps as simple as it seemed to me at first. Still, most days are quite interesting, and I've gotten to know people in the community too!

Extract 7

I spend around an hour every day in the car travelling to and from work. I used to quite enjoy it, but I like it less and less these days. First, I struggle to see on the motorway at night. The lights to me just make things blurry, and don't help me to see the roads, but what drives me mad is when someone moves along at the speed of a snail and you're stuck behind them. It just makes me late, and I hate arriving late to work as I can never find a spot to park… it gets so busy in the mornings.

Extract 8

Looks are important. And sometimes we all need a little help. But never fear – you're not alone! At Shine-nez, we're the specialists at making your place look great! Just call us now on 0560 65 65 65 and take the stress out of your day. No job is too big or too small. We charge by the square metre. See our price list on our website shine-nez.com and quote the code SHINERADIO, that's SHINERADIO, for 10% off your booking. Remember, let us take on the hard work while you just Shine! Contact Shine-nez now on 0560 65 65 65.

Practice test 2: Transcript | Part 2 (page 140)

Extract

Hello and welcome. I'm Hugo Mitchell. I work in road safety, which is why I am here to talk to you today. Before I start, I'm not focusing on drivers in this talk. I'll mainly be looking at how we can all walk the streets safely. Pedestrians need to be much more careful than other road users, so it's important that we all know what we should do.

I've worked in this area for ten years, so I hope you will find this talk useful. As well as my own knowledge, I'll look at data from surveys of over twelve towns, so we can see what's working and what isn't. In fact, I'd like to start with that.

We all need to take care when walking on the streets, but there are some areas where we need to be more careful. These areas are known as accident black spots. They are where accidents are more likely to happen. From the data, accidents are twenty times more likely to happen when people are going across the road without using a crossing. So, that's a key thing to remember – always cross where you are supposed to. But you still need to be careful. Even if you want to cross the road at some traffic lights, it's not enough to wait for the lights to change colour. Try and make eye contact with the driver coming near you. Make sure they can see you and are slowing down *before* you start walking.

Time of day is also important to think about. More accidents happen at night, mainly because of the eyesight of drivers and how well people can be seen. So, think about bright clothing if you go out in the evenings, and try to stay near streetlights. Also, never wear earphones when walking at night.

Another big factor is whether the streets have pavements. A road without pavements is five times more dangerous.

Road planning by councils helps lower risk, of course, but it's not enough. This all might seem like common sense to you, but the data shows that human error is by far the biggest reason accidents happen. Other factors, like mechanical or road faults, play a very small part in all this.

I also want to mention what the council has done to improve safety of *all* road users. They've been thinking a lot about making pavements safe. Streetlights have been installed in all of our major roads for years now, but they've also been planting trees along pavements to make them safer. The council are also thinking about changing road signs. They're looking at adding flashing signs to some busy areas, so drivers will slow down and be more careful. I'm unsure about this myself. Some people think that lights will make signs more obvious, but this could also be distracting. I wonder what they will decide to do about this, especially considering how much these lights cost.

So, what's in the future for road safety? Well, technology plays a big part. Self-driving cars will change everything, but will take a while to become common. One thing that is already available and popular is the Driver Attention Monitor, or D.A.M., in cars. This can tell us about tiredness and bad driving, and these things use something called artificial intelligence, or AI. This will make a big difference to safety. AI is often looked at with suspicion by the general public. However, for us in the safety industry, it could lead to almost zero accidents. And I'd like to think that's what everyone wants, really.

Practice test 2: Transcript | Part 3 (page 140)

Extract 1

I was actually terrible at art at school. I had no skill at all – but I always enjoyed it, even though I didn't pass the subject. When I was in my 40s, I decided to take a course and try again. I'd been working as an accountant for years, and I'd got a little bored in my job and just wanted to do something completely new and fun. I've got to say it's been incredible. The people there are so supportive, and I've learnt that actually I'm not so bad at art! I don't think I'll ever be Van Gogh, but it's certainly turned into a new hobby now!

Extract 2

Actually, I'm already an artist. I used to do it as a hobby, but it slowly grew into a job for me as I sold more and more pieces. Being successful doesn't stop me learning, though. I was self-taught, so I took a class because I doubted myself and my skills a little bit. I found out that I *was* doing things correctly, but, most importantly, I felt better about myself at the end. I think I was always worried that I wasn't properly trained, but now I feel ready to take any opportunity that comes my way in life!

Extract 3

I remember doing lots of art projects at school and always enjoying them, but, like many people, art wasn't a big part of my adult life. I actually came back to it when I retired, as although my life was quite relaxing it was also a little boring! I wanted to fill in some spare time with something new. I persuaded a group of friends to take an art class with me, and we had a fantastic time – and I learnt so many new skills! I've also now got the opportunity to show some of my art in the local town hall. I'm not sure I'm brave enough to do it, though, to be honest!

Extract 4

Art is an important part of my life, but it's more a hobby for me than anything. When a friend said she loved my work and would like me to design something for her garden wall, well, I was honoured. I'd done some initial designs on paper, but I took a course about wall art, just to make sure I was using the correct materials. It really helped, and lots of people have said that they love it! I'm wondering now if I should turn this hobby into a career. Although, I think it's quite a competitive area, so I'm not sure I'll be good enough.

Extract 5

I used to love art, but I hadn't done it for a long time when I decided to take the course. I remember the first day feeling so uncomfortable – I knew nothing! But I knew I had to take the course as I had such a busy schedule – I wanted something to calm me down, and I could save time just for myself. That's difficult to do when you have three children! I've actually improved a lot, and I now help the kids with their art projects. I'm thinking of meeting up with a group of local artists soon, just to ask them what it's like to dedicate themselves to art full time, and maybe get ideas for the future!

Practice test 2: Transcript | Part 4   (pages 142–143)

Extract

Interviewer	Welcome to the show, Chris Walker and Louise Franklin. I'm delighted that you could join us today on 'Learning for Sport'. Before we talk about your jobs as instructors, can you tell our listeners how you got into rock climbing?
Woman	Well, Chris has been climbing ever since he saw a TV show about it when he was a teenager, but for me it's quite a recent hobby. A few years ago, I was having coffee with a friend and she started telling me about a book she'd read which was written by a female rock climber. Her achievements sounded amazing. At that time, I was looking for a challenge, so I thought I'd give it a try.
Interviewer	Rock climbing sounds great as a hobby, but what made you want to teach others how to do it – Chris?
Man	I've done a few courses over the years – some good, some not so good. On the last course I was particularly impressed with the instructor's technique. I learned a lot and realised that training to be an instructor is a great way to improve.
Woman	I couldn't agree more! I just wanted to be like the instructors at my local climbing club – they make everything look so easy. When I found out that I could go on a course and learn to be like them, it seemed like a logical choice.
Interviewer	What are the requirements to become an instructor?
Man	You need to take one of the qualifications offered by Mountain Training, the organisation in the UK and Ireland that manages six different instructor courses.

	The courses relate to different types of climbing – so, for example, some are for climbing on indoor walls and there are others for assisting rather than leading climbs. Whichever one you choose, you must demonstrate that you have enough experience otherwise they won't let you on the course. Remember that they want everyone to pass, so it's better to wait until you're definitely ready.
Interviewer	It sounds tough. What was it like on the course?
Man	I really enjoyed all the physical aspects, but I think that's because I was quite fit before I started. Unfortunately, I found out that I'm really bad at giving instructions to other people. I worked hard to improve that on the course and I'm much clearer now.
Woman	For me, it was more about managing my response to situations. When we were practising with beginners, I worried that some of them would never be able to master even the basics. But the course made me realise that's not true – as long as you have a good instructor! Now I enjoy helping people achieve their goals, whatever their level and however small their goals might be.
Interviewer	Do you have any suggestions for people who want to try rock climbing?
Woman	Don't just do one session because you might be a little afraid if you've never done any climbing before. The ropes and equipment can be confusing. Commit to a short course so you can see yourself improving and gaining in confidence. I think a lot of people give up before they've overcome that initial fear. These short courses are designed to give you a real taste of climbing without spending a lot of time and money.
Interviewer	Thank you, Louise, that's great advice. And Chris, how would you say that rock climbing has affected or influenced your life?
Man	Well, I mostly climb outside, and I think getting out in nature is something that we should all do more often. Also, helping others improve their climbing skills and allowing them to believe in themselves makes me feel content because it's really worthwhile.
Interviewer	Yes, I can imagine. Now I'd like to move on to…

Practice test 3: Transcript | Part 1

Extract 1

Hi Daniel, it's Julia here. Unfortunately, I'm afraid I've got a bit of a problem right now. My daughter isn't feeling very well, and I think it would be best if I stayed home to look after her. I don't think it's serious enough to go to the doctors, but I'd rather not leave her alone. Anyway, that means I won't be able to make it for the tennis match later this evening. I was wondering if you're free on Friday instead? I know there are some free courts because I called the club earlier to check. Let me know what you think.

Extract 2

Man   I'm looking for a house which is near the local primary school because I have two young children and I'd like it if they could walk to school.

Woman   Okay. Well, we have a few options for you – some are large flats and others are houses.

Man   Okay, let me stop you there because I definitely want somewhere with a garden. Besides the children, we also have a large dog and it needs constant exercise. It's much easier to just let him outside rather than taking him to the park three times a day!

Woman   Okay, we have this house here. You can see from the photos that the garden is quite large – there's even space for a barbecue!

Extract 3

Where we are standing now formed part of the castle gardens. They were added during the 18th Century, but the castle itself is older. It was built a hundred years before that. As you can see, the gardens have different walled sections, which suggests that they were extended over the years. Although we are not sure, it is likely that this happened during the 19th Century when the castle was also extended. You can see that the walls built at this time were constructed from different-coloured bricks. Now, let's move on to the next part of the tour, the entrance to the castle…

Extract 4

Man   I've been looking at the travel options for the conference next week. Unfortunately, if we want to get there by 9.30 we're going to need to take the early train.

Woman   Okay, that's fine. I don't mind getting up early for a conference, but are you sure about getting the train? Isn't it expensive? Why don't we take the bus instead because it doesn't take that much longer?

Man   Well, I think the train is worth the money, to be honest, because it's much more comfortable. There's more room for your luggage and the seats are bigger. I mean, we have to pay extra if we want to reserve a seat, but I'd rather have a pleasant journey.

Extract 5

Woman I really hope it goes well after all the preparation we've done.

Man Well, I'm certain that the team will really enjoy it. We've put considerable time and effort into it, and I think that afterwards everyone will understand much more about the project and why it is essential for the company. Remember that everyone in the audience actually *wants* to hear what we have to say so there's no need to be nervous in my opinion.

Woman Well, I just hope that they think it's interesting and they ask some good questions at the end as that will make me feel like it was all worth it.

Extract 6

Man Do you think we should take the kids to the new pizza restaurant on Saturday night?

Woman I'm not sure. They've already eaten pizza once this week – remember, we had pizza delivered after their swimming class on Tuesday – so I think I'd prefer it if we had something a bit healthier.

Man We could get them to look up a new recipe and order the ingredients online. I think that would be a nice way to spend the evening together as a family, and we don't need to spend lots of money at a restaurant.

Woman Okay, that sounds like a better idea.

Extract 7

Man I was wondering if you'd like to come to the flower show that's taking place in Trenton next Saturday? I realised the other day that the summer food festival starts here tomorrow, which probably means the city centre will be full of tourists, so I was thinking of getting out of town while it's on.

Woman Ah, that sounds like it might be interesting. I'd planned to see something at the theatre on Saturday evening, but now I'm not convinced that's a great idea.

Man Okay, so how about I drive and pick you up at about ten o'clock, which will give us plenty of time to get there.

Woman Great. I'd really appreciate that.

Extract 8

I know lots of people think that students shouldn't be allowed to take their mobile phones into the classroom these days. They think it's a waste of time or that students will just be checking social media all the time. And yes, it's true that they can distract some students from their work, but this only happens if the teacher doesn't manage things properly. Mobile phones can be used for looking up facts and checking information, so they can actually help in lots of different ways. As long as teachers know how to get the best out of mobile phones, I don't have a problem with them in class.

Practice test 3: Transcript | Part 2 (page 148)

> **Extract**

Hi everyone. My name is Paula, and today I'm going to talk about video games – why people play them and what makes a good game. As someone who works in this area, I think I know something about the topic.

Lots of people have studied video games. And while psychologists say that a sense of connection often attracts people to playing them, it's not people's main motivation – that's the sense of achievement they get. There's nothing quite like succeeding in a game and making it to the next level! But gaming also produces lots of benefits, too. One example of this is that people often feel in a calm but concentrated state when they're playing, and this helps with stress levels. It can also take us away from everyday life.

Of course, there are so many types of games, so not all of these factors will apply to all games, but we certainly think about these kinds of things when making a game. Let me tell you how it's done. The first place that development starts is in the Concept Team. They really have the initial idea, and then my team, the art department, tries to think of the look and feel of the game.

Some initial drawings are done, and also we think about the technology we need. At this stage we also make a plan. We identify the competition and define the audience for the game. This is very important because the game design and the rules of the game will change depending on this.

We then work on making a test version of the game. This is just to see how it works. Then we show it to the managers. We wait for approval of the test version, and they tell us what the budget is and what changes they'd like, so we can start work on a complete version. We also get a suggested release date for the game here.

This leads us to the main production, and this is when all the hard work starts. There's a lot to be done before the game is ready to sell. It's a team effort between the designers and technical people. This isn't a series of stages, like many development projects – it's more like a cycle, with feedback and changes going from the design to the technical team and back again. Towards the end of production, the marketing team also starts working on the game. There used to be lots of huge adverts for new games, on things like movie trailers, but we tend to use social media instead these days. This means we can target advertising at people playing similar games. You can't do that in mass-media adverts, and it's also a lot cheaper!

Our company doesn't stop working when the game is sold, either. We've got a huge support team in two countries offering support in twelve different languages. Gamers get really annoyed if something isn't working for them, so this also helps us identify anything that needs to go back to the development team. There are always a couple of small errors that appear in the final product. We aim for none, because we want the game to sell well, be enjoyable and have few, if any, complaints.

And that's the end of the process really. Developing video games is a great job and I'd recommend it to everyone. It's so creative, for everybody that works in the company, and if your games are good it can be very well-paid! If you'd like more information about working in this area, and what qualifications you might need, please do ask me.

Practice test 3: Transcript I Part 3

Extract 1

I am a nursery schoolteacher, and I just love getting to know the children in the first year. They've never been away from their parents all day before, and it's interesting to see how they manage it. Some of them find it difficult to share toys, for example, while others really enjoy having new interactions. I always get a nice feeling when I work out the games and activities that interest each child. This is because it can have a big impact and help them settle into the whole-school environment. They know they've got something fun to do even if they're a bit nervous.

Extract 2

My work as a martial arts instructor gives me a lot of pleasure, especially in children's classes. We have to spend a lot of time helping students manage their emotions. Martial arts are all about control, and instructors need to understand that children do not think about this in the same way as adults. I spend a lot of time reading about how children's brains work so I can be a better instructor. We get different personalities, and some children are very sure of themselves while others can be very shy. It's important to get them all working together in classes so that they can *all* improve their skills.

Extract 3

I teach children who are 11 and 12 years old, and for me this is the best age group because they are about to become teenagers. You can start to see their characters taking shape at this age. Some are obviously confident and like to lead in class, whereas others are better at listening to their friends or problem-solving. It's so interesting watching them all interact with each other. At this age, school also starts to become more interesting because they have different classes for subjects like geography and history. I notice that they ask a lot more questions at this age!

Extract 4

I run an art club for young people on Saturday mornings. It's become really popular recently because quite a lot of parents think that the school curriculum is too academic these days. They want their children to have more time to do creative activities. A lot of the children want to make digital pictures using all sorts of different software, so I'm trying to get more confident using all this stuff. What I love is that the internet is full of ideas about how to use them in class. Last week I found a website full of games with some excellent instructions for teachers.

> Listen for synonyms and different ways to say the information in the options.

Extract 5

I am an educational psychologist, and I work with children who have learning difficulties. My job can be challenging, but people like me can make a big difference to families. I regularly communicate with parents, and it's great to explain the improvements that I've seen in their children's learning – it doesn't matter if they are small. All children have talents and abilities, but for some the traditional classroom just isn't the best place for them to learn. I have a lovely quiet room with toys and games. It's a place where children can learn about themselves and discover what they like to do.

Practice test 3: Transcript | Part 4 (pages 150–151)

Extract

Interviewer	Natasha Evans is the manager of a successful sports shop. Today she's going to tell us all about her role in the company and her views on selling sportswear. Welcome, Natasha. Tell me: what is your daily life like at work?
Woman	Well, my job covers all the usual things that you'd expect from a shop manager. I check and order stock, manage the staff and so on. But something that people might not expect, though, is that I have to make sure I know what's going on in the world of sport. The changing fortunes of teams and players effect what we stock in the shop. This changes from year to year. I read about it a lot, but I don't watch a lot of sport.
Interviewer	What's the age of most of your customers?
Woman	Teenagers and young people make up a large proportion of our customers. If you asked most people what modern teenagers are into, they'd probably say 'designer trainers'. And this is true to some extent, and what's most popular with this age group are names like Nike and Adidas. We sell more of those items than football shirts. Young people are the consumer group that dictates our stock, especially the quantities of things we buy for the different departments – sportswear, shoes, equipment and so on.
Interviewer	I imagine that selling sportswear is very competitive. How do you manage to keep your customers happy?
Woman	Well, most successful shops have a wide selection of items that are connected to popular sports like football and tennis and swimming. However, I think that listening to customers and getting to know them is what has made this shop stay profitable. For me, that's how you make sure customers keep coming back. It works better than having lots of discounts or loyalty cards.
Interviewer	Is there a part of the business which interests you from a personal perspective?
Woman	Yes, there is actually. I've recently started a business course which is very interesting. I didn't study business at university, and I'd like to update my skills and knowledge. Right now, we're focusing on the habits of different types of shoppers. After that we're going to study sustainability and the labour conditions

	in large factories around the world. I think the last one will be the most interesting for me.
Interviewer	And talking about working conditions, what are your staff like?
Woman	Oh, they are all great and work really well as a team. Some of them want to make a career out of working in sport. If they want to do this, going to conferences is vital – so we have a budget for that. Networking is great because they can meet inspiring people and get ideas for their future. Although I do sometimes have to remind them about the boring administrative tasks.
Interviewer	Is there any aspect of your job that you find challenging?
Woman	Despite the fact that we have a lot of regular customers – and I have a great team – planning is always a challenge. Things can change easily if someone is sick or we suddenly run out of an item. I've started using a planning tool on my laptop to predict possible problems and solutions.
Interviewer	And finally: do customers' tastes change a lot in sportswear like in other aspects of fashion?
Woman	Well, sportswear brands are becoming much more popular now. People wear them as a form as casual clothing now not just for playing sports. No one would have thought about doing this a few years ago. But beliefs about what clothing is appropriate for certain situations is not the same as it was.
Interviewer	Hmm. That's very interesting. Well, thank you, Natasha…

Practice test 4: Transcript | Part 1 (pages 154–155)

Extract 1

Man   Hmmm. I think we've got a problem with the car. What do you think this yellow light means?

Woman   I'm not too sure. It might be something connected to the engine? We should probably take it to a mechanic so they can check it.

Man   I'd rather not. I've got to take it to a meeting tomorrow – I've got to drive there – and we'll never get the car back from the mechanic in time.

Woman   Well, we can't ignore it. What if I just try to look it up online? Perhaps then we can see if it's serious problem or not.

Man   That sounds like a good idea. If it's bad, I promise I'll ask someone to look at it.

Extract 2

I remember how I felt on my first day at the job. I was so nervous! It's always hard when you start a job. You can't find anything, and you don't know what to do! But everyone around me was lovely. The nurses were so friendly and always offered me help when I needed it. Actually, it was working in the hospital then that persuaded me to study medicine. I mean, I was only answering enquiries and organising paperwork but working with the public like that made me realise that I really enjoyed helping people. Now, I've been a doctor for five years, and I absolutely love it.

Extract 3

It used to be much easier to go fishing in the area, but now there are fines if you fish in the wrong place. According to the local government, it's for our own safety but I don't think that's particularly true. I mean, we're still allowed out in boats to fish. That's far riskier than fishing on the shore. I understand that people think we need to maintain the number of fish in the sea, but wouldn't it be better to stop big companies that are fishing? I think the local government cares more about profits and how the area looks for tourists than us local fishermen.

Extract 4

Football management is a difficult job. There's a lot of money involved, and a lot of pressure. But nothing beats the excitement of match day. To me, it makes all the stress worth it. Lots of managers find the most exciting part is watching how the game changes, because obviously a big part of the job is making decisions during the match. But, for me, that time in the dressing room just before the match begins is particularly thrilling. What I say in that room can make players play better and make them believe in themselves. I think that this time can make a big difference.

Extract 5

Woman	I really cannot believe this! That novel was really special to me. I knew I shouldn't have given it to you in the first place!
Man	I'm honestly sorry. Look, it's got to be somewhere – these things don't just disappear.
Woman	When I gave it to you, I *did* tell you that I'd got it signed by the author, and it's been in my collection for years.
Man	I don't know what to say. I'll look again and if it doesn't turn up I'll get you a replacement.
Woman	Well, it's not going to be signed, is it? You may as well just forget it, but don't think I'm lending you anything else ever again!

Extract 6

I am pleased to be here today to talk about my newest novel *Flowers in Time*. Now, this book is quite different from my other novels, and I wanted to explain the reason behind this. For me, when I had the idea for the story I knew I had to write it outside of time order, so the novel jumps in time. One minute we see Jules, the main character, as a mother, the next as a teenager. This might make it a difficult read for some people, but I felt the story needed this, and I hope you agree once you read it.

Extract 7

I went to see the Brilston Quarter last week in the Central Hall. The tickets were half price for the last few days, so I thought: why not treat myself? It was much better than I'd expected, both in terms of the music and the musicians. You could really tell they were dedicated professionals, and they were absolutely spectacular in places. Although, I have to say they didn't look too comfortable under the lights of the stage. I think they were too hot – you could see them sweating! I'm glad I wasn't playing and was just relaxing in the audience.

Extract 8

Woman	People told me that the new shop in town is great, but I didn't think it was as good as it looks.
Man	I know what you mean. I went in last week, and it looks great from the outside, even though it's in that old building, but once you get in it's not very impressive. The shop assistants basically ignored me, and everything was so expensive too – and it didn't seem worth it.
Woman	Oh, I thought there were some cheap things in there, but I wouldn't buy anything. Not with the way they treat you in there.
Man	Yes, it's one of those kind of shops that thinks it better than its customers.

Practice test 4: Transcript | Part 2

> **Extract**

I'm always looking for new exciting challenges, so when I had the opportunity to go into a volcano, I knew I had to grab it. Most people perhaps wouldn't fancy doing something like that, and I can understand why people might get nervous about the idea. Not me, though. I was quite keen! And, after all, the volcano isn't active, so it's completely safe.

On my adventure, once I arrived at the nearest city, I took a bus to the parking area. From there I had a three-kilometre hike to the meeting point, which was next to the mouth of the volcano. It was quite a tricky walk to be honest because of the rocks, and I imagine it's easy to twist an ankle or something. The problem is the land isn't suitable for vehicles like cars, so it's walk or take a helicopter, which I didn't have the money for! And it's not any quicker than the hike when you take into account all the waiting around.

I managed to complete the walk in just under an hour. I wore good hiking boots, as I knew the land would be difficult. I didn't expect the changes in the weather, though. Preparation is really important, as one minute it's hot and the next you need to put on waterproofs – so you need to carry some different clothes, just so you're not caught by surprise.

At the mouth of the volcano, there's a group of guides who work there and will take you down. They fit you with the special equipment you need, like a harness, head lamp and helmet, but they also give you a safety talk, which was by far the most important thing. It prepared me for what I was about to do, and what to do if something goes wrong. If you go, I suggest you listen carefully to the guides.

There were four other visitors with me when I went. I expected us to go down in a lift like the ones that miners use in mines, but actually it was more like a lift for window cleaners. It was completely open with the volcano all around it. You could see everything! It was absolutely stunning.

I would definitely recommend doing this, even people with a fear of heights! It might sound strange, but you do feel completely safe. The one thing that might put people off, though, is the lack of room at the mouth of the volcano. The entrance is really quite small, but once you get inside, the volcano opens up into a massive space! And when you're down there, it's unlike any place you've ever been. We were allowed out of the lift at this point. I was worried that we'd have to stay in the group, all together and just listen to the guide, but actually, we could take photos and walk around – as long as we didn't leave the marked paths. My pictures don't really show how amazing the rocks were. There were all kinds of colours down there.

On the journey back up, I felt sad to be leaving and quite cold. Some of the guides were waiting for us at the top with hot lamb soup or hot chocolate. As I'm a vegetarian, I only had the latter – but it was so needed. It was actually quite cold and wet inside the volcano, so it was nice to have something to warm me up.

So, it was a really special experience, and so unusual. Most volcanoes close up so you can't enter them, but thankfully this one is empty. Nobody knows why it's open inside – it remains a mystery. But it's a treasure of natural beauty, and I feel very lucky that I have seen it.

Practice test 4: Transcript I Part 3

Extract 1

We know much more about global environmental concerns compared to our parents, and I try to do my best to help. There are lots of environmental projects here, and I try to take part in as many as I can. For example, me and my kids help pick up rubbish around the village and I help plant new trees. I think it's really important to take part in things like this to ensure your local environment stays pleasant. I believe if you think of that first, then eventually it will make the whole world a better place. That's really what we all want!

Extract 2

I do my best to protect the environment, but I worry it's not enough. I'm always concerned how what we throw away goes into nature, especially the oceans, and I'm sick of seeing plastic in the streets. That's why I do my best to use up everything I have; I always use things that are recyclable and I also try to buy second-hand if I can. I also try to encourage others in the community to do the same thing, although I don't think they always listen. I suppose some people see it as a big effort to help the environment.

Extract 3

We often recycle at home, and we've also got an electric car. I don't really enjoy recycling things – it's so annoying having all those different bins – but my husband and kids say it's the right thing to do, so I just do it. Electric cars are just the most popular ones to buy these days – in my circle of friends, anyway. For us, it's actually turned out cheaper to run than our old car, which is an advantage. It's also much less noisy than the old car. I remember the days when cars polluted a lot – you could even feel it when you breathed – so things have become so much better really.

Extract 4

I try to do my best to help the environment, although I'm sure it's not enough. I'm not always very good at recycling, for example. I do, however, bike everywhere and I never take a plane – so I don't think I pollute the environment very much. Now I'm a dad, I think it's important to think about this kind of thing – mainly for my daughters and their future families. I think my parents' generation didn't do much at all, and now we're starting to see the effects of that. It would be a shame if my generation didn't do enough either.

Extract 5

There are so many different ways we can care for the environment, and it's hard to do everything. I think we've just got to do small things that make a difference. I try to encourage bird species in my garden, because I know some of their populations are in trouble. My children also love helping me with this – it's such a great family activity! Of course, lots of people choose to reduce their waste or save energy, and these are great things to do too. I'm more concerned with waste in general, but I think it's such a big issue that it's hard to know where to start!

Practice test 4: Transcript | Part 4 (pages 158–159)

Extract

Interviewer	Today, I'm talking to Rachel Parkinson, who's a theme-park psychologist. I didn't even know that was a job! So, Rachel, what made you decide to specialise in theme parks?
Woman	Well, I'd always been a theme-park fan, but I'd also been interested in psychology. When I saw a talk that someone did on entertainment psychology at a conference, I realised I could combine those two things. And I'm glad I did. It's really interesting, and the field has excellent pay and conditions.
Interviewer	So, why do people go to theme parks?
Woman	For lots of different reasons, really. Groups of friends tend to go because it strengthens their relationships, but parents often take their children so they can all have something to look back on. It's nice to think back to a really fun day, and I've got to say, theme parks *are* a lot of fun for everyone!
Interviewer	Well, yes, they are fun, but they can also be quite terrifying. Especially the big rides, don't you think?
Woman	Well, I'm not so scared of them to tell you the truth. To me they're really exciting, and some of those rides are truly impressive. But did you know that recent research shows that most people go on them because they are stressful, but in a positive way. They make us feel really good afterwards, and actually boost our mood!
Interviewer	But it's the waiting and thinking about what's going to happen. I'm afraid it's not for me. In fact, I've known people waiting for those big rides for hours! Why do people bother?
Woman	Ha ha! Well, actually the parks design the waiting times, because it makes the rides look like they're popular. You would think it would make people decide to not go on the ride, and try something else, but actually psychology shows they enjoy the tension of thinking – just like you: what's going to happen!? Of course, there does need to be a limit to that waiting time, and we always try to make sure people aren't put off.
Interviewer	Hmm. That's really fascinating. What else can you tell us about theme-park psychology?
Woman	Well, one interesting thing is the use of colours that are used. We always think quite carefully about this. Red shows excitement and aggression, but soft blues, greens and greys give people a feeling of calm. We make sure we use these

	colours in the right places, so customers feel more, or less, energetic, depending on if they're at the rides or near, say, the café or shops.
Interviewer	Talking about the shops. I imagine they make theme parks a lot of money. Are they also considered carefully?
Woman	You'd be surprised how much we think about the customers' shopping experience. Children tend to always want to go into the shops, so we always make sure there's plenty of toys around, but we also want customers to buy things before they leave. Some theme parks actually lower the temperature in the shops if they want to sell more expensive items like coats and jackets. And it works! These kinds of sales can make a big difference.
Interviewer	Wow! That's incredible. So, how would you sum up the experience of visiting a theme park?
Woman	We think carefully about the visitor experience, but this is for business purposes. We manage absolutely everything. People think they are making choices, but we've kind of designed everything so we know exactly what they're going to do. Our priority is the success of the park, but of course we want people to have a great experience, full of sounds, fun and emotions too. It's always important that they come back!

A digital platform for Cambridge exam preparation

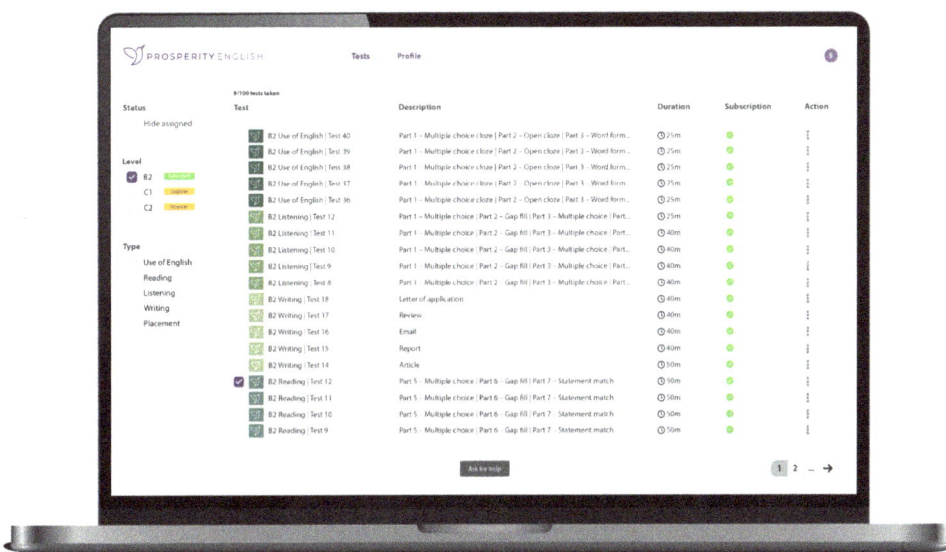

Prosperity English provides ample opportunities for repetitive practice, allowing you to reinforce your learning and improve your exam skills steadily.

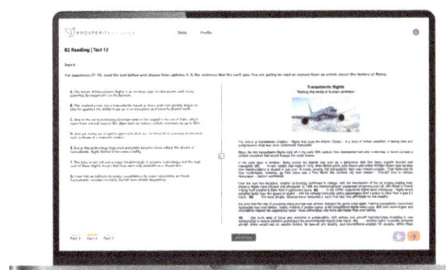

Try it for free

www.prosperityenglish.com

50% promotional discount code:
JOENGLISH50

www.ingramcontent.com/pod-product-compliance
Ingram Content Group UK Ltd.
Pitfield, Milton Keynes, MK11 3LW, UK
UKHW062045180426
11947UKWH00030B/2055